EDUCATIONAL INFRASTRUCTURE
FOR
BIOTECHNOLOGY IN INDIA

By the same authors
Economic Liberalisation and Public Enterprises

About the Authors

Professor R.K. Mishra is currently Professor and Dean, Institute of Public Enterprise, Hyderabad. He is a graduate of International Management Programme, SDA Bocconi, Milan, Italy. He has had research stints at London Business School and Maison Des Sciences De L'Hommes, Paris. He has been the recipient of British Council, Commonwealth, IIAS, IASIA, ICSSR, UGC and UN Fellowships. He has taught at the University of Bradford, United Kingdom and was a visiting Professor at Maison Des Sciences De L'Hommes, Paris. He was on action research at North-West Province of South Africa at the invitation of DFID, UK. He is Vice-President (Asia), International Association of Schools and Institutes in Administration, Brussels.

B. Navin is currently Knowledge Manager at the Centre for Good Governance, Hyderabad. He has worked for his doctoral thesis on Asset Pricing Behaviour in Indian Stock Market. He has been associated with the Asian Development Bank Project and at the Institute of Public Enterprise, Hyderabad.

P. Geeta is currently Knowledge Manager at the Centre for Good Governance, Hyderabad. She has completed her doctoral study on Memorandum of Understanding in Public Sector Enterprises in India. She has also worked in the area of Social Safety Net for the State Level Public Enterprises in Andhra Pradesh.

Ms. Ch. Lakshmi Kumari is currently Research Associate at the Institute of Public Enterprise, Hyderabad. She is a resource faculty to various MBA programmes. She has been associated with various training programmes organised for national and international agencies.

EDUCATIONAL INFRASTRUCTURE FOR BIOTECHNOLOGY IN INDIA

With Special Reference to Andhra Pradesh

R.K. MISHRA
B. NAVIN
P. GEETA
CH. LAKSHMI KUMARI

CONCEPT PUBLISHING COMPANY, NEW DELHI-110059

Cataloging in Publication Data—DK
Courtesy: D.K. Agencies (P) Ltd. <docinfo@dkagencies.com>

Educational infrastructure for biotechnology in India : with special reference to Andhra Pradesh / R.K. Mishra ... [et al.].
p. cm.
Includes bibliographical references.
Includes index.
ISBN 8180693201

1. Biotechnology—Study and teaching—Government policy—India. 2. Biotechnology—Study and teaching—Government policy—India—Andhra Pradesh. 3. Biotechnology—Research—India. 4. Biotechnology—Research—India—Andhra Pradesh. I. Mishra, R. K. (Ram Kumar), 1948-

DDC 660.607 22

ISBN 81-8069-320-1

First Published 2006

Published and Printed by
Ashok Kumar Mittal
Concept Publishing Company
A/15-16, Commercial Block, Mohan Garden
New Delhi (INDIA)

Phones : 25351460, 25351794
Fax : 091-11-25357103
Email : publishing@conceptpub.com

PREFACE

Just as the physical infrastructure of bridges, roads, and other public works is required to support the Nation's economic vitality, the infrastructure for biotechnology education and research is critical to the research enterprise. Existing support for infrastructure accounts for a very insignificant amount of the total government investment in biotechnology research.

Neglect of infrastructure needs ultimately results in decreased productivity and lost opportunities. The government's commitment to meet these needs should be long-term, stable, and allocated on the basis of merit. The present study tries to capture the scenario of infrastructure for biotechnology research, education and industry in Andhra Pradesh. It describes the status of current infrastructure, including both physical and human resources, needed for biotechnology research.

The Study touches upon the importance of developing instrumentation centres available to researchers from government, academia, and all industry sectors. The Study further highlights issues related to funding for the acquisition of state-of-the-art equipment for biotechnology research.

The Study underscores the need for new and expanded repositories to hold and preserve the many specimens and large amounts of data crucial to biotechnology research.

The Study emphasizes that innovation and progress in biotechnology depend on the existence of a supportive, thriving intellectual climate. Broad-based education is needed to provide a continuing supply of well-trained researchers. The challenges of biotechnology require problem solving that crosses traditional disciplinary boundaries. Programmes to provide retraining and interdisciplinary training of scientists and technical/vocational staff are essential.

The Study suggests that government agencies should expand training grants that link the disciplines underpinning biotechnology (e.g., biochemistry, microbiology, structural biology, genetics, ecology engineering) and should support technical/vocational education to provide a workforce familiar with the concepts and tools of biotechnology.

Training and career development in the infrastructure area promises the greatest overall impact on biotechnology. Programmes are needed to enhance public literacy concerning biotechnology, as well as to attract and retain students in biotechnology-related science and engineering through pre- and post-doctoral levels, and to retain individuals with experience in other disciplines for careers in biotechnology.

The Study points out to the general needs in undergraduate, graduate, and continuing education programmes:

- Training is needed at the interfaces of biotechnology-related disciplines involving biologists, biochemists, computer scientists, physicists, chemists, material scientists, geologists, hydrologists, and engineers.
- Training is needed in theoretical and computational biology.
- Training should include study of non-traditional organisms for biotechnology.

The Study points out the need for training programmes for mid-level technical personnel. Several agencies have programmes to recruit and train independent investigators for the future. Relatively little attention has been given, however, to the large number of mid-level technical workers that will be required to transfer research results to applications. This type of training should not be ignored in planning for future personnel needs in biotechnology. Specialized vocational training for biotechnologists is only one approach, however, a broader solution may lie in encouraging colleges and universities to reinstate laboratories as integral parts of basic science courses.

There is also a need for education and training to promote general scientific literacy. A training issue-specific to agricultural biotechnology is the need to maintain support for scientific progress by assuring a knowledgeable public. Programmes are needed to develop and disseminate educational materials about biotechnology and foster open discussions of new developments and applications.

PROF. R.K. MISHRA
DR. B. NAVIN
Hyderabad **DR. P. GEETA**
CH. LAKSHMI KUMARI

ACKNOWLEDGEMENTS

The study entitled, ***Educational Infrastructure for Biotechnology in India with Special Reference to Andhra Pradesh*** is a joint effort of the team consisting of Prof. R. K. Mishra, Director, IPE, as Adviser, Dr. P. Geeta and Dr. B. Navin, Ch.Lakshmi Kumari as Team Members.

To understand the existing infrastructure facilities for biotechnology education and the future requirements, the Study Team interacted with a number of experts in the field of biotechnology research, education and industry. The conclusion drawn based on such interactions and feedback has been documented as part of the Study.

We are grateful to Padmashree Prof. M.V. Rao, Chairman, AP Netherlands Biotechnology Programme, Biotechnology Unit, IPE, for his kind support and guidance. We thank Prof. G. Pakki Reddy, Coordinator, BTU and Professor of Economics, IPE, for placing confidence in our team and assigning us the above project.

We acknowledge the support of BTU faculty members and staff, especially Dr. P.S. Janaki Krishna, Dr. MLN Rao and Dr. Anji Raju, who provided valuable inputs for the Study, especially, during the conceptual stages of the project. We thank Ch. Lakshmi Kumari, Research Associate, IPE, for her support.

We extend our thanks to Dr. V. P. Gupta, Adviser, Department of Biotechnology, New Delhi, and Dr. C.R. Bhatia, Former Secretary, Department of Biotechnology, Government of India for providing valuable insights for the Study.

We thank the staff and faculty of IPE for their support and assistance in the conduct of the Study.

ACKNOWLEDGEMENTS

CONTENTS

LIST OF TABLES

EXECUTIVE SUMMARY

The present Study on "Educational Infrastructure for Biotechnology in Andhra Pradesh", attempts to assess the current status of infrastructure—physical, financial and human resources—for biotechnology education and research in Andhra Pradesh. The Study bases its analyses and findings on the primary information received through a questionnaire survey addressed to the universities and educational institutions, research laboratories, and R&D establishments in the public as well as the private sector. It also draws upon the secondary information available in the form of existing literature on the subject and the periodic surveys conducted by the Department of Science & Technology, Government of India and Government of Andhra Pradesh. Information and ideas received through personal interviews with eminent experts, leading scientists, industrialists, and educationists, provides substantial content and direction to the Study findings.

The Study contains 7 chapters dealing with critical aspects related to educational infrastructure for biotechnology including the Government policy at the Central and State level, the state of S&T in India, financial resources available and related constraints, status of S&T manpower and future requirement, courses, fellowships, being offered by various universities and institutions, industry-academia collaboration, and physical infrastructure for bio technology education and research. The concluding chapters provide a summary of the responses from questionnaires and interviews received from different categories of respondents, and suggestions and recommendations based on the responses and other formal and informal inputs received during the course of the Study. A gist of all the chapters is presented below:

Biotechnology in India: An Overview

This chapter introduces to the strategic significance of the biotechnology to the Indian Economy, outlines institutional set up and budgetary allocations for the biotechnology, discusses the changing role of the Department of Biotechnology in the development of biotechnology, provides an overview of the steps initiated for the human resource development and training the biotechnology personnel and enumerates the efforts undertaken by the various state governments to popularise the biotechnology in India.

Over the years India has developed strengths in biotechnology in public sector institutions. In-graduation from Biotechnology Development Board to Department of Biotechnology (DBT) in late eighties was a decisive step to address a wider canvas in biotechnology. In these years DBT has emerged as a major force to direct biotechnology developments in India. Further, the involvement of various agencies dealing with this technology has further helped in developing technology capability at various levels. The size of the industry is estimated to have grown to $1.5 to $2.5 billion between 1999 and 2002.There are two major research centres in India working on stem cell line research.

The achievements in biotechnology in India could become possible only because the government took early initiatives for setting up institutional infrastructure for human resource development. As of now more than 62 universities and institutions are engaged in biotechnology training and education related programmes. Efforts are being made to link up human resource development programmes according to industry requirements, and in fact, academic institutions are also being encouraged to work in close tandem with industry, India has attached greater importance to bioinformatics. DBT has set up 55 centres for bioinformatics, which have been developed as a strong information network. They are linked with databases and networks around the world. The whole range of new initiatives to support biotechnology programmes at Indian Institute of Technology and at Jawaharlal Nehru University are aimed in that direction. The micro propagation technology parks at TERI, New Delhi and NCL, Pune have served as an important interface between the industry and the developers of the technology in the areas of plant tissue culture. National Centre for Plant Genome Research and National Brain Research Centre are some of the recent additions. However, it is difficult to estimate precise R&D allocations to many of these centres. The budgets of major funding agencies like CSIR/ICMR and ICAR give only an aggregate picture. Therefore, there is an urgent need to launch a detailed survey to collect specific biotechnology related allocations at the individual institute/laboratory level. Apart from this, DBT or some other such agency should urgently initiate an exercise for data collection either on its own or through specialised sectoral agencies.

Policy on Educational Infrastructure for Biotechnology in India

The purpose of this chapter is to discuss educational infrastructure for science and technology (S&T) in India with special reference to Andhra Pradesh, biotechnology policy of the Government of India and the Government of Andhra Pradesh and the need for Human Resource Development for the growth of biotechnology.

Andhra Pradesh Scenario

The Government of Andhra Pradesh Biotechnology Policy Paper 2001, highlights the existing network of research laboratories, and the existing pool of scientific and technical manpower, indicates the intention of the Government to provide high quality infrastructure at reasonable cost with integrated services to biotech manufacturing units by setting up a series of Biotech Parks throughout the State, and points out to the critical mass existing in Andhra Pradesh for the Biotech Industry.

The chapter further points out that human resource development would determine the success or otherwise of the biotechnology advances. Not only the policy framework has to be adequate but its implementation and the focus have also to be appropriate to enable the biotechnology advances yield the desired results. The requisite human resource development alone could ensure a resounding success on each of these parameters.

Multi-Dimensional Analysis of Educational Infrastructure *vis-à-vis* the Biotech Sector

This chapter outlines the various dimensions related to educational infrastructure in biotechnology, and the SWOT (Strengths Weaknesses, Opportunities and Threats) analysis pertaining to biotech sector in India.

SWOT ANALYSIS OF INDIAN BIOTECH SECTOR

Strengths

- Trained manpower and knowledge base
- Good network of research laboratories
- Rich Bio-diversity
- Well developed base industries (e.g., pharmaceuticals, seeds)
- Access to intellectual resources of NRIs in this area
- Extensive clinical trials and research – access to vast and diverse disease populations
- Bio-diversity – India's human gene pools offer an exciting opportunity for genomic research. Unique and diverse plant, animal and microbial bio-diversity also provides exciting research opportunities

Weaknesses

- Missing link between research and commercialization
- Lack of venture capital
- Relatively low R&D expenditure by industry
- Image of Indian industry—doubts about ability of Indian companies to develop original products for international markets

Opportunities

- Large market
- Export potential
- Base for contract research for international companies due to rising costs of R&D abroad
- Large number of patients covering wider range of diseases – clinical research/trials

Threats

- Danger of anti-biotech propaganda gaining ground
- IPR policies

The dimensions of educational infrastructure for biotechnology are variegated and require a multi-pronged approach for their fuller comprehension in the absence of which it would not be possible to formulate appropriate paradigms to provide competitive edge to biotechnology industry in India.

Trends in Biotechnology Education and Training

This chapter presents an analysis of the trends in biotechnololgy education and training.

The major points which emerge are:

1. The present trend in the manpower coming out of the PG courses organised in various universities by DBT is following a quadratic model due to the increase in the number of institutions offering this programme over the last 10 years.
2. The post-M.Sc. & M. Tech Industrial Training is received by only a handful of students compared to the number of students who pass out every year. Even out of the students who receive training only a few get jobs.
3. Similarly, it is seen that the facilities for training large number of technicians is not available. Facilities are available only to train an average 20 technicians per year.

4. The participation of industries in the short term training programmes is very low compared to that from universities and research institutes.
5. The number of BT Associateships being provided now gives opportunities for about 20 scientists per year to work in National laboratories and about 20 to work overseas.

Suggestions to increase production of manpower with the requisite qualification include:

- Universities could be informed by DBT of the possible shortages and initiate or strengthen courses which would be able to produce personnel of adequate numbers with required training.
- Mid-career training and retraining through short and mid-term training courses would be participated by the user industries who would have a say in the designing of the training courses and also cosponsor these thereby having an opportunity to get the manpower with desired skills.
- The DBT should give very serious attention to increase facilities to train more technicians which is the need of the hour.
- Getting the Indian biotechnologists trained in BT, working abroad back through offers of attractive opportunities to invest and work.
- To facilitate efforts to increase rates of absorption of trained manpower for the jobs for which they are trained.
- Increase jobs at the level of training like initiate courses in many colleges for post-graduate diploma courses. This effort while increasing the number of personnel of required skills/qualification available for the industries would also increase the number of jobs available for PGs in courses related to BT for the purpose of training.

Infrastructure for Biotechnology Education: An Analysis of Survey Responses

This chapter is intended to present an analysis of responses received from some institutions engaged in biotechnology education research in Andhra Pradesh and other parts of the country.

Andhra Pradesh

The responses received in the case of Andhra Pradesh could be divided into two parts: written responses and oral responses. The written responses were received from the Department of Micro Biology, University College of Science, Osmania University, Hyderabad; New Science Degree and PG College, Kakatiya University, Warangal; Biotechnology Division, Andhra University, Visakhapatnam; Indian Immunologicals Limited, Hyderabad; Shantha Biotechnics Pvt. Limited, Hyderabad and Centre for DNA Fingerprinting and Diagnostics, Hyderabad. The oral responses came through interaction with the Indian Immunological Limited, Hyderabad; Department of Biotechnology, University of Hyderabad, Hyderabad; Department of Biotechnology, Acharya N.G. Ranga Agricultural University, Hyderabad. The oral responses received in the case of Andhra Pradesh have been grouped with the oral responses received through interaction on the state of the biotechnology education existing in general in the country.

The following points emerge from the responses provided by the Universities in Andhra Pradesh:

- The capital expenditure for infrastructural facilities ranged from nil in few cases to around Rs. 30 lakhs which included equipment cost, lab furniture, chemicals, glassware, computers etc. Over the period 2000-01 and 2001-02, the level of expenditure was more or less the same.
- Various courses offered in biotechnology and allied subjects by the universities include—Agriculture Biotechnology, Plant Biotechnology and Animal Biotechnology, Industrial & Engineering Biotechnology,

Downstream Processing in Biotechnology, Biochemistry & Microbiology, Transport Phenomena and Separation Processes, Adsorptive and Chromatographic Separations, Laboratory Techniques in Biotechnology, Genomics, Bioinformatics, Medicinal Biotechnology, Biosafety, Ethical and Proprietary Issues, Microbial Technology and Biodiversity.

- In most of the cases, the syllabus is revised once in three years and annually in few cases. Although students have been consulted in most cases on the revision of syllabus, there is not much progress in this direction. Similarly, interaction with the industry is at a meagre level. Although there are tie-ups with the industry, there is no active collaboration going on and at the most the students are provided with a few projects which are very preliminary in nature and does not lead to any serious application.
- The strength of the faculty ranges from three to seven per department and over the one-year period 1999-2000 to 2000-2001, the figures are more or less the same. In most of the cases, there is a formidable presence of supporting staff.
- Most of the respondent universities have faculty visiting them from various related departments such as botany, zoology, environmental sciences, pharmaceutical sciences and statistics. Experts are also drawn from the industry and foreign universities.
- Refresher courses are being offered by some universities for lecturers of affiliated colleges. Other extension programmes are being conducted through consultancy and guest lectures outside. Most of the respondents feel that such training programmes help in updating the existing knowledge on the subject, increase the intensity and level of interaction with the industry and provide inspiration for carrying out research projects. It also provides an opportunity to scientists, policy makers, and beneficiaries to come to a common platform and exchange their views.

- It has been felt that bioinformatics, genomics and proteomics need to be added to the existing curriculum.
- In nearly 50 per cent of the cases, there are no scholarships for pursuing biotechnology and related disciplines in the universities. There are studentships given in few cases sponsored by the DBT, Government of India. In one case, the university has provided one scholarship each for rank holder at post-graduate/M.Sc., M.Phil and Ph.D. levels.
- Universities have followed the tradition of organizing national and international seminars and symposia on biotechnology wherein experts from other countries also participate. This has been a common trend across all the universities.
- Active interaction with Industry and R&D support is present in one or two cases and lacking completely in most of the cases.
- The lab facilities currently existing in the universities include, tissue culture lab to conduct protocol development for propagation, microbiology for industrial microbiology research, fermentation lab for enzyme production, large scale fermentation, food biotechnology lab for enzyme modifications, applications etc., pharmaceutical biotechnology for synthesis of chiral compounds using enzymes, microbes, plant tissue culture for synthesis of flavour, perfumery compounds using plant tissue culture, affinity chromatography and separations lab for separation and purification of metabolites, enzymes and developing new ligands for chromatography, supercritical and other extractions lab for extraction, purification of metabolites by supercritical, ultrasonic and other recent techniques, biotech lab for industrial biotech research and downstream processing.
- Some of the major scientific equipments listed out by the respondents include HPLC, HPTLC, GC, UV Spectrometer, Electrophoretic Apparatus, Super Centrifuge, Environment Chamber, Ultra Low Deep Freezer, Gaulin

Homogenizer, Bioreactor and Photo bioreactors, Sonifier, Liquid Chromatography Unit, Lab Scale and Pilot Scale Fermentors (15 to 65 litres, Chemap, Electrolab etc.), Elcctron Microscope, Bio-profile System etc.

- Only a few universities have separate computer hardware and software facilities for their biotechnology centre. Among them only a couple of universities have provided access to internet and LAN in their biotech units.
- Most of the universities are subscribing biotech related journals and magazines. However, online and offline computer databases are non-existent but for a few universities.
- As per the responses, under the repositories for biotechnology research, the following shared resources for biotechnology research are available at few universities: nucleic acid probes, DNA clone libraries and microbial stock cultures.
- Only one university has reported the status of placements of students in biotechnology. The number of placements at the post-graduate level average out to 6 in the research labs, 3 in the industry, 4 in affiliated colleges. The placement scenario has been similar for 1991-2000 and 2000-2001 in this case.

The following points emerge from the responses provided by the research institutions and industrial R&D units dealing with biotechnology:

- Across all the research institutions and industrial R&D units, an increasing trend in the scientific and technical personnel involved in biotechnology research has been observed.
- However, the level of industry-academia interaction and industry support to students is very low. As far as training programmes are concerned, there is no effective mechanism for students to be sent for training in industries and research institutions. Barring few exceptions such as

CSIR Labs, more effective mechanisms need to be evolved so that younger talent is acquainted at the right time with the requirements of industries *vis-à-vis* their career development and ambition.

- In order to plan biotechnology well, the industrial R&D units have the perception that the syllabus should aim at imparting fundamental knowledge in modern biology covering molecular biology, cell biology, microbiology, biochemistry, and genetics as an integrated approach. It is also essential that the students have adequate knowledge of physics and mathematics required to study the topics covered in biotechnology.
- The major scientific equipments available at the R&D units include automatic computer controlled bio-reactors of various capacities from 10 L to 100 L for microbial and mammalian cell culture, provided with state-of-the-art accessories for exhaust gas analysis, perfusion and online nutrient and metabolite analysis. Cross-flow filtration systems of various types such as membrane, hollow fibre and ceramic for handling filtration processes upto a volume of 1000 L, continuous centrifuge for handling large-scale separation processes upto a volume of 500 L, homogenisers including a bead-mill and a high-pressure homogenizer for pilot scale cell disruption, sophisticated computer controlled chromatography systems for laboratory and pilot scale protein purification along with axial and radial flow and expanded bed columns of various sizes, pilot scale lyophilizer for aseptic freeze-drying, dry heat and steam sterilizing equipment, florescence and phase-contrast microscopes with camera and video attachments, scanning densitometer, gel documentation system, UV-VIS Spectrophotometer, Spectroflouimeter, HPCL, GC, Liquid Scintillation Counter, Oligonucleotide Synthesizer, Thermocyclers, Tunable UV-VIS Plate Reader, Automated DNA Sequencer, SD200 Spectral Karyotype System, Beekman XL-100 Ultra Centre, UV-VIS Scanning Spectrophotometer, AB1392 DNA synthesizer, ABI Prism

7000 Real Time PCR Machine, ELISA & PBR Equipment, Fluorescent Microscopes, Spectrophotometer and CO_2 incubators.

- In most of the cases, Internet facility is accessible to all the research centres. Scientific and technical data availability has been indicated for areas such as federal and state regulations on Biosafety and reference standards for quality assurance of biotechnology based measurements.

Responses received in the form of informal discussions and personal interviews from policy makers and academicians are as follows:

Policy Makers

The policy makers feel that universities should take the lead in making the biotechnology education meaningful and relevant. In their opinion the biotechnology education needs sophistication at molecular level. They suggest that any biotechnology department should have a minimum of five faculty members dedicated to develop the biotechnology programme which should have a maximum intake of ten to twenty students. While during the three semesters of a post-graduate programme theory and practicals could be covered, the fourth semester should be exclusively devoted to project work and summer training. The labs should have internet facility, all expensive consumables and biochemicals and network with industry. Guest faculty should be generously invited to associate with biotechnology courses. They also suggest that besides promoting the general master's programme in biotechnology, specialized masters programmes should also be promoted with agricultural biotechnology, marine biotechnology, and nuero sciences. The biotechnology department should help in solving the problem of staffing the departments with capable faculty. The biotechnology department should provide a core grant of Rs. 24 lakhs over a period of five years for strengthening the faculty. The policy makers also suggest to institute specialized

PG diplomas in biotechnology such as genetic engineering, transgenic food, etc. Short-term training programmes should be run for carrier scientists. A biotechnology-industry programme of six month's duration is suggested for creating job opportunities and such a programme should be funded by the industry. Post-doctoral fellow programmes should be commenced in the lines of Indian Institute of Sciences, Bangalore. India need to create world class manpower to give a push in the biotechnology programmes.

Academicians

The academics in the field of biotechnology suggest that the biotechnology education should provide broader and specific knowledge. For instance, the academic institutions in Andhra Pradesh around seacoast should specialize in marine biotechnology whereas such institutions in Hyderabad should specialize in molecular aspects of biotechnology. The universities should employ really talented people who have access to relevant literature, internet and gateways. No faculty should be allowed to have more than three projects. The academic institutions should also organise themselves for better management equipments. The jobs should be provided on contractual basis. The faculty should inculcate the habit to interact with other colleagues. Enough money should be provided for the acquisition and maintenance of equipment and instruments. The funding agencies should handle the maintenance. The budget authorities should not starve the biotechnology departments of funds and impose unproductive systems. The committees constituted to give a green signal for purchases of consumables should meet very frequently and not have such members who have no idea of biotechnology research and the cost of the equipments involved in carrying out the biotechnology research. The funded projects from the government have the tendency to place the government staff and such tendency should be avoided. The biotechnology education requires motivated teachers and staff possessing deep research inclination. The universities should promote collaborations. For uninterrupted supply of materials, universities should blacklist the firms that go back from their promise of supplying a given quality and quantity of materials at a specific time.

The educational infrastructure for biotechnology in Andhra Pradesh and the other states is in infancy. There is a scope for tremendous improvement in the areas of capital expenditure, academic inputs, information development, database creation and growth, shareable resources and placements. All the stakeholders need to play an active role to ensure the availability of enhanced infrastructure and access to the tools of information technology. A constructive institute-industry interface and public-private partnership could lead to a quantum change in the scenario. The academic institutions need to become pro-active and reorient themselves to get in line with the needs of time.

BT Education in India and Andhra Pradesh: Towards a New Framework

Biotechnology's broadest definition can be given as the application of all natural sciences and engineering in the direct or indirect use of living organisms or parts of organisms in their natural or modified forms in an innovative manner in the production of goods and services and/or to improve existing industrial process. The Biotechnology education is multi-disciplinary in nature. It is an integration of biological sciences with disciplines such as the chemistry, physics, information technology, engineering drawing, electrical and electronics, mechanical engineering, chemical engineering, etc.

After Information Technology (IT) boom, India with its large pool of scientific talent, world-class information technology industry, and vibrant pharmaceutical now seems to be shifting its focus to the most promising industry of the future, i.e., *Biotechnology*. India with its exploding population is a huge market for products and services. India offers a perfect base for the biotech companies which are looking for greener pastures.

Although biotechnology holds key to a brighter future of India, the biotechnology education does not reinforce this assertion. The biotechnology education suffers from a number of serious shortcomings as related to the content, spread, pedagogy, intake, admission systems and procedures, topicality, industry demands and the surveyor. The infrastructure facilities in terms of equipments, lab layout and the technicians continue to remain substandard. Though India has established a global outreach in biotechnology, it needs to consolidate the position both at home and abroad.

Suggestions and Recommendations

General Recommendations

- Evolving a specific policy on biotechnology education;
- Facilitating growth of a supportive, thriving intellectual climate for development of biotechnology education;
- Encourage research and higher education in biotechnology to provide well-trained professionals in biotechnology education;
- Initiate programmes to provide retraining and interdisciplinary training to scientists and technical and vocational staff;
- Provide adequate funding for improving facilities in universities and colleges across all the departments;
- Check the deterioration in existing facilities and lack of funds for new facilities for biotechnology research limits the progress;
- Coordinate efforts to upgrade research facilities in universities and educational institutions;
- Maintain operate high grade equipment and instrumentation to support research of high caliber which are expensive and difficult to acquire;
- Provide funding for state-of-the-art equipment for biotechnology research and make it available to the academic institutions;
- Arrange resource sharing facility for the institutions with research labs and industry groups;
- Organise programmes needed to enhance public literacy concerning biotechnology, as well as to attract and retain

students in biotechnology related science and engineering through pre- and post-doctoral levels and retain individuals with experience in other disciplines for career in biotechnology.

Admissions

- The number of students admitted in the biotechnology courses at all the levels far exceeds the sanctioned strength of the institution.
- Uniform norms to be laid out by the educational institutions with regard to the selection of candidates for various graduate and post-graduate course in biotechnology.
- The management of these institutions would ultimately be the deciding factor on the candidatures thus giving way to a dilution in the quality of the students at these courses.

Fee Structure

- The huge fee structures of the various biotechnology courses which vary from Rs. 5000 to Rs. 10,000 at the university offered courses and from Rs. 50,000 per annum to Rs. 1.2 lakhs per annum in private colleges affiliated to the various university deprives a financially weak student to join the course.

Infrastructure

- Mushrooming of biotechnology colleges to be stopped immediately.
- The infrastructure available in the educational institutions to provide instructions in biotechnology is not adequate to cater to the intake admitted.
- Excessive intake of students results in a decline in quality of the end product. Primarily, the infrastructure rarely allows the students to have hands on experience.
- These shortcomings lead to a turnout of biotechnology

graduates and post-graduates ill-equipped both in theory and practice.

- The academic audit wings in the universities should ensure the availability of the requisite lab space, instrumentation facilities and qualification of the teaching staff.
- There occurs at some stage a compromise to high standards, eventually resulting in deficiency of certain essential facilities.
- Ultimately it is observed that students are obliged to make do with facilities that fall short of their need and expectations.
- Further, no planned efforts are undertaken to nurture, develop and upgrade biotechnology department in terms of proficiency of teachers, lab facilities, and library and industry interaction.
- The lab facilities currently existing in the universities include, tissue culture lab to conduct protocol development for propagation, microbiology for industrial microbiology research, fermentation lab for enzyme production, large scale fermentation, food biotechnology lab for enzyme modifications, applications etc., pharmaceutical biotechnology for synthesis of chiral compounds using enzymes, microbes, plant tissue culture for synthesis of flavour, perfumery compounds using plant tissue culture, affinity chromatography and separations lab for separation and purification of metabolites, enzymes and developing new ligands for chromatography, supercritical and other extractions lab for extraction, purification of metabolites by supercritical, ultrasonic and other recent techniques, biotech lab for industrial biotech research and downstream processing.
- Some of the major scientific equipments listed out by the respondents include HPLC, HPTLC, GC, UV Spectrometer, Electrophoretic Apparatus, Super Centrifuge, Environment Chamber, Ultra Low Deep Freezer, Gaulin Homogenizer, Bioreactor and Photo bioreactors, Sonifier, Liquid Chromatography Unit, Lab Scale and Pilot Scale Fermentors (15 to 65 litres, Chemap, Electrolab etc.), Electron Microscope, Bio-profile System etc.
- Only a few universities have separate computer hardware and software facilities for their biotechnology centre. Among

them only a couple of universities have provided access to internet and LAN in their biotech units.

- Most of the universities are subscribing biotech related journals and magazines. However, online and offline computer databases are non-existent but for a few universities.
- As per the responses, under the repositories for biotechnology research, the following shared resources for biotechnology research are available at few universities: nucleic acid probes, DNA clone libraries and microbial stock cultures.

Scholarships and Assistants

- In nearly 50 per cent of the cases, there are no scholarships for pursuing biotechnology and related disciplines in the universities. There are studentships given in few cases sponsored by the DBT, Government of India. In one case, the university has provided one scholarship each for rank holder at post-graduate/M.Sc., M.Phil and Ph.D. level.
- Universities have followed the tradition of organizing national and international seminars and symposia on biotechnology wherein experts from other countries also participate. This has been a common trend across all the universities.
- Active interaction with Industry and R&D support is present in one or two cases and lacking completely in most of the cases.
- However, the level of industry-academia interaction and industry support to students is very low. As far as training programmes are concerned, there is no effective mechanism for students to be sent for training in industries and research institutions. Barring few exceptions such as CSIR Labs, more effective mechanisms need to be evolved so that younger talent is acquainted at the right time with the requirements of industries *vis-à-vis* their career development and ambition.

Placements

- Only one university has reported the status of placements of students in biotechnology. The number of placements at the post-graduate level average out to 6 in the research labs, 3 in the industry, 4 in affiliated colleges. The placement scenario has been similar for 1991-2000 and 2000-2001 in this case.

Biotechnology Education and Faculty

- The strength of the faculty ranges from three to seven per department and over the one-year period 1999-2000 to 2000-2001, the figures are more or less the same. In most of the cases, there is a formidable presence of supporting staff.
- Most of the respondent universities have faculty visiting them from various related departments such as botany, zoology, environmental sciences, pharmaceutical sciences and statistics. Experts are also drawn from the industry and foreign universities.
- Refresher courses are being offered by some universities for lecturers of affiliated colleges. Other extension programmes are being conducted through consultancy and guest lectures outside. Most of the respondents feel that such training programmes help in updating the existing knowledge on the subject, increase the intensity and level of interaction with the industry and provide inspiration for carrying out research projects. It also provides an opportunity to scientists, policy makers, and beneficiaries to come to a common platform and exchange their views.

Biotechnology Education and Faculty

Qualification and Workload

- Teachers teaching in most of the biotechnology courses are not those who have been appointed on a permanent basis but rather gathered from various departments.
- The problem is further compounded by the question as to how well qualified are most of these teachers to teach in biotechnology courses.

- Secondly, the workload, though in terms of norms is supposed to be 16 hours per week per faculty member, actually exceeds the norm by nearly 50 to 100 per cent mainly due to the requirements of lab work, lack of support from qualified technical staff and more number of students per batch than should be logically allocated.
- A post-graduate biotechnology class should have ideally a minimum of 10 to a maximum of 15 students. But this is very rarely the case. The need to make sure that the courses are run self-financed or secure a surplus, forces many academic institutions/institutions offering courses in biotechnology to admit a very large number of students.
- This reduces one to one interaction required between the teachers and taught which is so essential for this course.

Biotechnology Education and Faculty

Workshops and Refresher Courses

- The demand of biotechnologists as such in India has increased only, of late, in spite of the fact that research in this field has made in rods for quite some time.
- Senior teachers, specifically in this field, who would act as mentors to the newly admitted students are not very easy to come by making the task of the teaching staff cumbersome and difficult.
- The DBT and UGC have not mounted vigorously refresher courses for the teachers, which could help them orient and update them to the expectations.
- Infact, the biotechnology is one field that would require frequent refresher programmes owing to continuous advancement in research in this field.

Biotechnology Education and Faculty

Remuneration

- The lecturership packages offered in general in the science stream is by no means fair.

- At the outset, the courses like bio-chemistry, microbiology and biotechnology in most colleges are not government funded like those of botany, zoology, chemistry and physics so most of the teaching staffs are not permanent employees but are rather appointed on a temporary basis (more appropriately as contract employees).
- The contracts are usually drawn for the academic year and terminated when the colleges close for the summer vacation.
- The employees have to seek their own means of remuneration during this period. The renewal of the contract is decided entirely by the management and no explanations are offered whatsoever if a particular staff is not inducted back again.
- This shabby treatment meted out to members offers very little encouragement to young aspirants who wish to take up a teaching job in biotechnology.

Syllabus

- A comprehensive syllabus is a prerequisite for bringing in greater credibility for the course.
- The syllabus to be in tune with the latest development in biotech field to make the students employable and acceptable to the market.
- Need to create greater space for vocational education in biotechnology.
- A basic orientation course to be instituted to bring in continuity between the undergraduate and post-graduate course to familiarize the students to the curriculum, which is not offered by the universities.

Various courses offered in biotechnology and allied subjects by the universities include—Agriculture Biotechnology, Plant Biotechnology and Animal Biotechnology, Industrial and Engineering Biotechnology, Downstream Processing in Biotechnology, Biochemistry and Microbiology, Transport Phenomena and Separation Processes, Adsorptive and Chromatographic Separations, Laboratory Techniques in Biotechnology, Genomics, Bioinformatics, Medicinal

Biotechnology, Biosafety, Ethical and Proprietary Issues, Microbial Technology and Biodiversity.

- In most of the cases, the syllabus is revised once in three years and annually in few cases. Although students have been consulted in most cases on the revision of syllabus, there is not much progress in this direction. Similarly, interaction with the industry is at a meagre level. Although there are tie-ups with the Industry, there is no active collaboration going on and at the most the students are provided with a few projects which are very preliminary in nature and does not lead to any serious application.
- It has been felt that bioinformatics, genomics and proteomics need to be added to the existing curriculum.
- In order to plan biotechnology well, the industrial R&D units have the perception that the syllabus should aim at imparting fundamental knowledge in modern biology covering molecular biology, cell biology, microbiology, biochemistry, and genetics as an integrated approach. It is also essential that the students have adequate knowledge of physics and mathematics required to study the topics covered in biotechnology.
- Some of the cutting-edge modules that could be included in biotechnology education and training programmes are: Basic Biology (Microbiology, Cell Biology, Biochemistry, etc.); Introduction to Computation/Information Theory; Genomics; Proteomics; Introduction to Algorithms; Introduction to Artificial Intelligence; Introduction to Microarrays; Computational Molecular Biology; Fourier Transformation, Hidden Markov Models, Fuzzy Logic, Biopackages-BioPerl, BioJava; Molecular Modelling and Drug Design; Neuroinformatics; and Cheminformatics.

1

BIOTECHNOLOGY IN INDIA
AN OVERVIEW

This chapter introduces to the strategic significance of the biotechnology to the Indian Economy, outlines institutional set-up and budgetary allocations for the biotechnology, discusses the changing role of the Department of Biotechnology in the development of biotechnology, provides an overview of the steps initiated for the human resource development and training the biotechnology personnel and enumerates the efforts undertaken by the various state governments to popularise the biotechnology in India.

Introduction

In recent past, two major Indian economic sectors, viz. agriculture and industry have been getting exposed to an entirely new set of technologies. The developments in the area of biotechnology are particularly of great interest. This frontier technology becomes important in a developing country like India where agriculture, with stagnating productivity and crops confronting many biotic and abiotic stresses, aims for higher growth. The industrial sector is expecting a change in production profile with new molecules and new enzymes. These changes assume a different dimension in an Intellectual Property Rights (IPR) regime, where stronger instruments are being used for its protection.

However, the emergence of biotechnology is also accompanied by an intense debate on techno-protectionism *vis-a-vis* the role of nation-state in technological development. In this context, several issues pertaining to the role of government and space for public sector supported R&D have been raised. The rapid economic development in many developing countries, especially in South East Asian countries, has demonstrated that national technological capability remains a key factor in competitiveness. Many studies in the recent past have underlined the importance of country specific institutional mechanism as a determinant of technological capability.

The increasing role of knowledge in agricultural production and the growing challenge of environment management in particular have to be acknowledged. This trend suggests that it has become increasingly important to bring dynamism in the functioning of the science and technology system at the national level. While the existence of a strong physical infrastructure is necessary for the development of an effective S&T system, the critical factors remain the institutional set-up that supports this system and the cohesion between the overall developmental objectives and the R&D endeavours in different streams. In this context, one idea that emerges forcefully is the development and competence of public sector R&D institutions in the realm of frontier technologies. In this light, it is also important to have accurate information and reliable statistical data about developments in this sector as that can only provide right feedback for desired policy formulations.

Institutional Set-up and Budgetary Allocations

India is one of the first few countries, among the developing countries, to have recognized the importance of biotechnology as a tool to advance growth of agricultural and health sectors as early as in 1980s. India's Sixth Five Year Plan (1980-85) was the first policy document to cover biotechnology development in the country. The plan document proposed to strengthen and develop capabilities in areas such as immunology, genetics, communicable diseases, etc. In this context, referring to the Council of Scientific and Industrial Research (CSIR), the document suggested to ensure coordination on inter-institutional, inter-agency and on multi-disciplinary basis, full utilization of existing facilities and infrastructures in major areas including biotechnology. Programmes in the area of biotechnology included, tissue culture application for medicinal and economic plants, fermentation technology and enzyme engineering for chemicals, antibiotics and other medical product development; agricultural and forest residues and slaughterhouse wastes utilization and emerging areas like genetic engineering and molecular biology.

The existing national laboratories under the S&T agencies, such as Indian Council of Medical Research (ICMR) and Council for Scientific and Industrial Research (CSIR) had initiated several research programmes to fulfil the above plan objectives. At the top, an apex official agency, viz. National Biotechnology Board (NBTB) was set-up in 1982, to spearhead development of biotechnology. The NBTB was chaired by Member (Science) of the Indian Planning Commission and had representation of almost all the S&T agencies in the country, viz. Department of Science and Technology (DST), Council for Scientific and Industrial Research (CSIR), Indian Council for Agricultural Research (ICAR), Indian Council for Medical Research (ICMR), Department of Atomic Energy (DAE) and the University Grants Commission (UGC).

National Biotechnology Board (NBTB) was formed with the specific purpose of the identification of priority areas and for evolving a long-term plan for the country in biotechnology as well as to initiate and promote such activities as conducive for further development of various areas in biotechnology. The NBTB issued the "Long Term Plan in Biotechnology for India" in April 1983. This document spelt out priorities for biotechnology in India in view of the national objectives such as self-sufficiency in food, clothing and housing, adequate health and hygiene, provision of adequate energy and transportation, protection of environment, gainful employment, industrial growth and balance in international trade. Later in 1986, NBTB graduated to a full-fledged government department called Department of Biotechnology.

At present in India, there are six major agencies responsible for financing and supporting research in the realm of biotechnology apart from other sciences. They are Department of Science and Technology (DST), Department of Biotechnology (DBT), Council of Scientific and Industrial Research (CSIR), Indian Council of Medical Research (ICMR), Indian Council of Agriculture Research

(ICAR) and University Grants Commission (UGC), Department of Scientific and Industrial Research (DSIR). DST, DBT and DSIR are part of Ministry of Science and Technology while ICMR is with Ministry of Health, ICAR with Ministry of Agriculture and UGC with Ministry of Human Resource Development. DSIR is the funding agency for CSIR and both of them independently fund biotechnology related research programmes.

Table 1.1 shows that the allocations for all of these agencies have gone up in the last decade. Out of this, DBT is the only agency completely devoted to R&D in biotechnology. It is very difficult to estimate the total allocations for this sector *per se* from other aforementioned agencies as in some cases the allocations are not separately marked as allocations for biotechnology. Thus separately accounting for biotechnology becomes difficult. Table 1.1 gives a broad idea about total allocations by major Indian funding agencies to science and technology related projects and not necessarily to biotechnology alone. In case of UGC it gives a broad idea not only about S&T related projects but also about other research streams.

Table 1.1 : Budgetary Allocations of Major Funding Agencies in India

(Rs. millions)

Sl. No	*Agencies*	*1990-91*	*2000-01*	*2001-02*
1.	Department of Scientific and Industrial Research (DSIR)	131.3	9704	3625
2.	Department of Science and Technology (DST)	2588.9	7798	8240
3.	Department of Biotechnology (DBT)	655	1361	1863
4.	Indian Council of Agriculture Research (ICAR)	3236	13992	13837
5.	Indian Council for Medical Research (ICMR)	396	1470	1673
6.	Council of Scientific and Industrial Research (CSIR)	2351	9120	9322
7.	University Grants Commission (UGC)	3495	14070	14908

Source: Budgetary Papers of relevant years, Ministry of Finance, Government of India.

There has been a significant increase in Government of India's outlays for biotechnology over the past decade. Since the time of establishment, in 1986, the allocation for the Department has increased manifold. The budgetary allocations have gone up from Rs. 404 million in 1987-88 to Rs. 1,138 million in 1997-98 and by 2001-2002 it became Rs. 1,863 million. Though the current price allocation figures may not give a complete picture but the budgeted figure for 2002 shows a doubling of allocation to Rs. 2,356 million. Table 1.2 shows the budgetary allocation to Department of Biotechnology.

Table 1.2 : Budgetary Allocation to Department of Biotechnology

Sl. No.	*Years*	*Rs. in millions*
1.	1987-88	404
2.	1988-89	470
3.	1991-92	740
4.	1993-94	880
5.	1995-96	965
6.	1996-97	970
7.	1997-98	1138
8.	1998-99	1165
9.	1999-00	1201
10.	2000-01	1361
11.	2001-02	1863
12.	2002-03	2356

Source: Budgetary Papers of relevant years, Ministry of Finance, Government of India.

In India, the developmental allocations are generally made for five years under the National Five Year Plans. The Government has recently finalized the Tenth Five Year Plan (2002-2007). The Working Group on Science and Technology for the Tenth Five Year Plan, constituted by the Planning Commission, has proposed an outlay of Rs. 20,750 million for the period 2002 to 2007 (Table 1.3). This marks a sharp increase of 234 per cent from the budgetary provisions made during the Ninth Plan period (1997-2002) which totalled at Rs. 6,215 million only. The Vision Statement for the

Tenth Five Year Plan enumerates the proposal for human genome sequences, proteomics, structural biology and bioinformatics.

Table 1.3 : Allocation for Biotechnology under Five Year Plans

Sl. No.	*Name of the Scheme*	*Ninth Plan*	*Tenth Plan*
01	Biotech Facilities, Centres of Excellence and Programme Support	680.46 (10.95)	900.00 (4.34)
02	Research and Development		
	2.1 Agriculture Biotechnology	1651.26 (26.56)	550.00 (2.65)
	2.2 Medical Biotechnology	808.88 (13.01)	4130.00 (31.46)
	2.3 Environmental Biotechnology	128.72 (2.07)	200.00 (0.96)
	Total	2588.86 (41.65)	7280.00 (35.08)
03	Biotechnology for Societal Development	— —	250.00 (1.20)
04	Bio-Process and Product Development		
	4.1 Food Biotechnology	— —	250.00 (1.20)
	4.2 Microbial and Industrial Biotechnology	— —	250.00 (1.20)
	4.3 IPR and Biosafety	7.51 (0.12)	100.00 (0.48)
	4.4 Programmes merged with other heads	513.05 (8.25)	— —
	Total	520.55 (8.38)	600.00 (2.89)

The DBT has established a huge infrastructure for bioinformatics. There are almost 55 bioinformatics centres working as a strong information network in the country, linked with databases and networks around the world for easy access by large number of scientists. Similarly, the DBT has supported 51 courses at different academic institutions all over the country to meet the growing demand of skilled manpower in the country as discussed later.

The DBT has 17 task forces in different areas of importance

each comprising 12-13 experts who help in recommending and monitoring to R&D projects. The DBT has launched an innovative scheme of developing institutional clusters to exploit the institutional and academic synergies and economise on resources. Recently, micro propagation technology parks have been established at the Tata Energy Research Institute, New Delhi and the National Chemical Laboratory, Pune. They are serving as an important interface not only between the industry and the developers of technology in the areas of plant tissue culture but also among the academic institutions.

The DBT has taken special precaution to find crucial balance between different sections of society as far as technology absorption is concerned apart from promoting industrial development. It is supporting low-cost biotechnology adoption programmes for socially backward communities. The programmes include vermi-composting, use of organic manure, silk-worm rearing, mushroom cultivation, etc. Some training-cum-demonstration programme is also being supported for them. Efforts are also on for gender mainstreaming.

Changing Role of DBT

In recent times, DBT has taken up a proactive role in promotion of industry. DBT proposed a single window application-processing cell as part of a new regulatory system for the domestic biotechnology sector. The move formed part of the recent recommendations on biotechnology sector made by the Confederation of Indian Industry (CII). Besides recommending setting up of a single window application—processing cell at DBT, CII had also suggested a fixed time frame of 150 days for clearing new biotech proposals.

In this regard, CII had recommended a process whereby a new application would be sent by the single window agency to the Review Committee on Genetic Manipulation (RCGM), which in turn would be required to submit a scientific evaluation report within 60 days of receiving the applications.

Council for Scientific and Industrial Research (CSIR)

The Council for Scientific and Industrial Research was established in 1942. It is India's largest research and development organization. It has 40 laboratories and 80 field stations/extension centres spread over the length and breadth of the country. The total allocation for CSIR in the year 2000-01 was Rs. 9120 million, which is 13 per cent higher from 1999-2000 (Rs. 7940 million). CSIRs Centre for Cellular and Molecular Biology (CCMB) incubated India's first recombinant protein product from a private company, Shantha Biotech, a hepatitis B vaccine, and it has numerous industrial relationships, including a joint venture with Biological E and Amersham Pharmaciato build DNA micro-arrays.

CSIR proposes to continue programmes in the area of agro-biotechnology, industrial biotechnology, and toxicant identification control, with a strategy for controlled change in direction as dictated by market needs. Strategic alliances would thus be sought for programmes for understanding the processes, molecular genetics and control of gene expression, genetic manipulation of microbes, recombinant DNA products, engineering new protein molecules/ new chemical entities, development of immuno-diagnostics and biotechnology of prospective medicinal and aromatic plants.

Indian Council for Medical Research (ICMR)

Another major institution working in the area of biotechnology is the Indian Council for Medical Research (ICMR) under the Ministry of Health. It is the apex body in the country to promote, coordinate and formulate biomedical and health research. Central Government gives full maintenance grant to the Council, to research in communicable diseases, contraception, maternity and child health, nutrition, non-communicable and basic research.

The total allocation for ICMR from the Central Government (Ministry of Health) was Rs. 1470 million in 2000-01, which was 21 per cent higher over the allocation of the previous year, that is 1999-2000 (Rs. 1160 million). The Council is also engaged in research on tribal health, traditional medicine and publication and dissemination of information. In the year 2001 ICMR has launched a major programme in the field of genomics (vector, microbial, human) with the initial allocation of Rs. 500 million. One of the major areas of focus is the disease susceptibility gene identification, especially for, communicable diseases like leprosy, tuberculosis, and communicable diseases as rheumatic fever or genetic diseases as thalassaemia. ICMR has established four centres for developing molecular medicine at All India Institute of Medical Sciences (AIIMS), New Delhi, Sanjay Gandhi Post Graduate Institute of Medical Sciences (SGPGIMS), Lucknow, Jawaharlal Nehru University (JNU), New Delhi and Post Graduate Institute of Medical Education and Research (PGIMER), Chandigarh. Apart from this, ICMR has also established six biomedical informatics units in different parts of the country. It has proposed an allocation of Rs. 1000 million for the Tenth Five Year Plan.

Indian Council for Agriculture Research (ICAR)

In India, agricultural research is being spearheaded by the Indian Council for Agricultural Research (ICAR) under the Ministry of Agriculture. The Council is engaged in conducting research in the field of agriculture, soil and water conservation, animal husbandry, fisheries, dairying, forestry and also agricultural education. The allocation for ICAR from the Ministry of Agriculture was Rs. 13,990 million in 2000-01, which was Rs. 12,060 million in the previous year. It has several research laboratories all over the country conducting research in biotechnology, besides using traditional breeding techniques for different research projects.

ICAR has established a National Research Centre on Plant Biotechnology (NRCPB) at the Indian Agricultural Research Institute (IARI), Pusa, New Delhi, which is fully dedicated to work on plant biotechnology. Annual expenditure over the projects at NRCPB is Rs. 150 million. Apart from this ICAR has also supported two research networks, combining ICAR and even non-ICAR research laboratories to work on crops like rice, cotton, brasica and brinxal. ICAR is also implementing a World Bank supported programme called National Agriculture Technology programme (NATP) through which huge allocations have been made at different research laboratories for strengthening infrastructure for biotechnological research.

ICAR has also collaborated with DBT and Rockfeller Foundation to jointly launch a National Rice Biotechnology Network (NRBN) in 1988. This project helped in evolving a culture of collaboration among different institutions, which has led to publication of several international papers in established journals. This network put together plant breeders and molecular biologists on the one hand and also provoked interests of private sector in R&D. For instance, Mahyco and Rockfeller Foundation worked together on identifying the relevant genes for saving Indian rice from brown plant hoppers. In this collaborative effort, interaction was not limited to private entities only. It is between private and public sector organisations also. Several universities also have tie ups with private sector organisations. For instance, Tamil Nadu Agricultural University (TNAU) attempted joint trials with Monsanto on weed resistance in soil. TNAU was partner in monitoring the BT Cotton field trials of Mahyco-Monsanto alliance. TNAU is also holding in exploratory talks with Rasi seeds (it is also in alliance with Monsanto) to conduct and monitor field trials of BT crops. Similarly, rice research work at National Research Centre for Plant Biotechnology has attracted business interest of companies like Nath Seeds Ltd. and JK Agri-genetics.

Human Resource Development and Training

The National Biotechnology Board had launched an integrated short-term training programme way back in 1984, to cope up with growing demand for highly trained manpower. In the first phase (1984-85), 5 universities were selected for initiating M.Sc./M.Tech programme in this multi-disciplinary area. Subsequently, in 1985-86 and 1986-87, the DBT has added 8 universities/institutions for M.Sc/M.Tech/Post-doctoral teaching programmes. Subsequently, DBT was entrusted with the responsibility of evolving curriculum for biotechnology courses and meet the demand for human resources in the field of biotechnology. In 1986-87, a model system of post-graduate/post-doctoral teaching in biotechnology in 7 universities/institutions was launched. Some of the specialised M.Sc. courses in marine and agricultural biotechnology were launched in 1988-89 at 3 universities. In 1992-93, DBT supported a five year Integrated Programme in biochemical engineering and biotechnology in Indian Institute of Technology, Delhi and a post-doctoral programme at Indian Agricultural Research Institute, New Delhi.

Now, DBT is supporting 20 M.Sc. courses in general biotechnology, 4 in agricultural biotechnology, one each in medical and marine biotechnology while couple of diploma courses in molecular and biochemical technology. The total intake of students in the various post-graduate courses supported by the DBT in the country is around 550 per year. As a part of restructuring of the post-doctoral research and training programme, DBT has scraped the on going programme with different institutions and has given this responsibility to Indian Institute of Science (IISc), Bangalore. This is to ensure competitive attitude and quality output in the life sciences. It is being proposed that IISc would award up to 75 fellowships of two-year duration in different streams of biotechnology.

DBT is also supporting overseas associateship and short-term training courses for at least 22-25 scientists in a particular year for exposing Indian scientists to newer trends in R&D. This helps working researchers and scientists to upgrade their knowledge and research areas of interest. In this context, services of Biotech Consortium India Limited (BCIL), New Delhi, a DBT floated organisation, are also being used to bridge the scientific knowledge of DBT supported associates and industry requirement. The State Governments are also exploring various options to finance higher education in such advanced technologies. Recently, Karnataka government has established an Institute of Bioinformatics and Applied Biotechnology (IBAB), in collaboration with ICICI Ventures to offer a post-graduate course in bioinformatics on its International Technology Park campus.

As part of a wider effort for capacity building in institutes of higher learning, full-fledged departments of biotechnology are being set-up. The Indian Institute of Science, Bangalore, Indian Institute of Information Technology and Management, Gwalior; and select Regional Engineering Colleges are setting up departments of biotechnology. The All India Council for Technical Education (AICTE) has already approved B.Tech. programmes in biotechnology in eight engineering colleges and has since been advised to develop a model curriculum for undergraduate programmes. All the new departments will have undergraduate, post-graduate and doctoral programmes. Special funding will be provided for the purpose in the Tenth Five Year Plan. Apart from expanding teaching of biotechnology at higher educational institutions a separate module on biotechnology would also be integrated with the school curriculum. The Department of Biotechnology of Government of India provides the necessary outline of this module so that the National Council of Education Research and Training (NCERT) and the Boards of School Education would be accordingly advised.

Indian University Grants Commission has come out with a scheme to promote higher centres of learning at one place and assist them as much as possible. In this regard, Delhi based Jawaharlal Nehru University (JNU) has been identified by the UGC as centre for excellence in the areas of genomics, genetics and biotechnology. The University has received funds to the tune of Rs. 300 million and is planning to start a new integrated M.Sc./ Ph.D. programme in life sciences and biotechnology and is setting up a modern animal house for experiments. Efforts are also being made to upgrade equipment and library facilities. The new integrated programme in life sciences will reduce the time taken by a scholar to complete his Ph.D. by at least within two years. Now the scholar will not be required to undergo a separate M.Phil programme. JNU is aiming at 10 seats for the integrated course and another 20-25 seats in the School of Life Sciences. The university has so far received 40 proposals for possible projects, which can be pursued by them in these fields in the future. Out of the funds that JNU has finally managed to get from the University Grants Commission on its selection as the University with potential for excellence, Rs. 100 million have been set aside for upgradation of facilities and equipments. The rest of the Rs. 200 million would help University to subscribe to some of the 8,000 online journals, both in the field of science and social sciences. Besides this, JNU also announced recruitment of more researchers. The tie-ups with industry are also likely to grow. For instance, researchers at the Centre for Biotechnology (CBT) at Jawaharlal Nehru University in New Delhi have been working for four years on a recombinant anthrax vaccine and soon would start Phase clinical trials in collaboration with Panacea Biotech Ltd. (New Delhi).

To sum up, there are almost 30 universities offering Masters of Science in Biotechnology through a joint entrance examination being conducted by the Jawaharlal Nehru University (JNU). Apart from this Goa University is offering a two-year Master of Science course in Marine Biotechnology, while All India Institute of Medical Sciences (AIIMS) offers a similar course in medical biotechnology. There are a couple of institutions offering Post Graduate Diploma Courses in Molecular and Biochemical Technology. Indian Institute of Technology (IIT) at New Delhi and Kharagpur offer a Five-Year integrated course in Biochemical Engineering and Biotechnology. There is a Post MD/MS Certificate Course in medical biotechnology being offered by Post Graduate Institute of Medical Education and Research, Chandigarh and Sanjay Gandhi Post Graduate Institute of Medical Education and Research, Lucknow.

Medical Biotechnology

The companies in medical biotechnology in India can be divided into three broad categories. One is that of small startup companies that have indigenously developed biotech products, e.g., Shantha Biotech and Bharat Biotech. Then there are large companies, which have started responding to biotechnology and have in fact incorporated biotechnology in their work plan, for instance, Dr. Reddy's Laboratory (DRL), Ranbaxy Laboratories and Wockhardt Ltd. The third group has start-ups, which are all set to emerge as Contract Research Organisations (CROs). Largely, their work comes from TNCs.

Then there are companies like Biocon India which may not fit well in this kind of classification as they have an established presence in the industrial biotechnology (the fermentation sector) and a growing presence in the pharmaceutical sector, so eventually accompany our first and second category. Biocon set its sights on biopharmaceuticals and using its capabilities in a wide range of lei-mentation technologies by 1995. Two years on, Biocon established Helix Biotech Pvt. Ltd.—a wholly owned subsidiary to develop its biopharma operations, which began with a range of anti-cholestrol statin drugs. Another subsidiary of this company, Clinigene International, was set up to initiate longitudinal clinical studies in select disease segments. Thus there is a synergy-based expansion, Biocon is now recognised as the country's leading biotech conglomerate.

Shantha Biotech

This is one of the leading examples of our first category of firms—small start ups with their own biotech products. Shantha Biotech has the credit of developing India's first world class Hepatitis-B vaccine and making it available at one-third of the prevailing market price of imported vaccines. This company has an active biotechnology programme since 1994. Now Pfizer Ltd., the major pharma TNC, has obtained the first refusal rights from the Hyderabad based Shantha Biotechnics Pvt. Ltd. for exclusively marketing the products to be developed by the latter in future. Earlier, Pfizer had entered into a co-marketing agreement with Shantha Biotech for marketing the latter's recombinant DNA vaccine for Hepatitis-B. Shantha Biotech is currently in advanced stages of discussion with one European pharma major and about three US based pharma companies for its research projects. The company plans to research on protein purification, molecular cloning and expression of native and synthetic genes. Shantha Biotech will also be offering polyclonal and monoclonal antibody development and formulation of certain types of vaccines. Shantha Biotech has developed in-house expertise in recombinant DNA technology and is very strong in development of cell lines for development of recombinant products. The company has invested Rs. 100 million in the biotech facility with external funding (from Bank of Oman).

Dr. Reddy's Laboratory (DRL)

Some of the companies like DKL have grown in the recent past. It was established in 1984. DRL is a big pharmaceuticals company and now is setting up biotech production facilities as per the US FDA specifications. The company has also identified biogenerics as significant market area which is estimated at $14 billion. It has pegged its brand value at Rs. 9,160 million as against last year's value at Rs. 2,850 million. The biotechnology facility includes setting up of three class 10,000 bulk recombinant protein production suites and new formulations facility as well. The biotechnology business would cover therapeutics, vaccines and diagnostics. DRL has a research alliance with Centre for Cellular and Molecular Biology (CCMB), Hyderabad. DRL has also established a research subsidiary in Atlanta called Reddy US Therapeutics Inc., as well as a contract research subsidiary that will focus on genomics.

Ranbaxy Laboratories

Ranbaxy, India's largest pharma company with sales of more than $500 million in the year 2000, also views innovation in biotechnology as key to its future. It is one of the oldest post-independence firm founded in 1968. The company has branched out from creating new formulations of existing drugs and has half a dozen molecules under development. Ranbaxy has collaborations with several U.S. and European companies to develop new formulations and technologies. For example, Ranbaxy and Ventura Ltd. (Bath, U.K.) announced in 2001 that the Indian company's Ranbaxy B.V. subsidiary (the Netherlands, Antilles,) will develop oral formulations using Ventura's controlled release drug delivery technology, with Ranbaxy providing clinical development, scale up, manufacturing and marketing expertise. Ranbaxy has set a model in India in terms of drug development. The model suggests that develop a molecule upto the level a domestic company can afford to do generally upto the first phase of the clinical trial and then outsource it to a leading MNC for further development and later on explore the possibilities for marketing tie-ups.

Wockhardt Ltd.

Wockhardt Ltd. established nearly four decade ago, is the fifth largest pharmaceutical company of India. Wockhardt has grown at over 20 per cent annually for the last 5 years. In the year 2000, it acquired Merind from the Tata's and besides Wallis Laboratories, a company in the UK, apart from entering into marketing alliance with the American Sidmak Labs. The company is formulating its biotechnology strategy around these initiatives. It has decided to split its business into two separate entities. Wockhardt Ltd. will remain as a pharmaceutical company while the new entity would focus on Life Sciences only. The new company (the name of which has yet to be finalized) will have all the other businesses, namely hospitals, nutrients, IV fluid and agrovet (Crop protection). The R&D activity is also being categorized into three divisions. The first division concentrates on developing new bulk drugs (Novel drug delivery system (NDDS) and generics. The second division concentrates on recombinant biotechnology. At present, the second division is focusing on technology absorption with the assistance of scientists from abroad. The third division is dedicated for discovery of new molecules. Wockhardt is expected to come out with its first investigational new drug (IND) in anti-infective therapeutic segment by the end of 2002.

At present, the turnover of CROs is very close to $100 million. The major companies in this category are Quintile India, Lambda, Welbech, Lotus and SIRO Clinpharm Ltd. Indian scientists from leading institutions are now actively floating companies, for instance, two scientists from Indian Institute of Sciences (IISc), Bangalore have floated a company called Metahelix Life Sciences with $1.5 million venture capital funding. The company would focus on providing contact research services in genomics, molecular markers and bioinformatics, to begin with and eventually developing new molecules on its own.

Initiatives by State Governments

In recent past several State Governments in India have launched different initiatives to attract biotechnology industry to their respective states for instance, Tamil Nadu has announced its biotechnology policy in September 2000, while Karnataka followed suit in February 2001. In the same year Andhra Pradesh was seeking to leverage its strengths in the pharmaceuticals, agriculture and IT services to put it at the forefront of the biotechnology race among the various State Governments. Not surprisingly, the States have extended similar concessions. already available to the IT sector.

Andhra Pradesh (AP)

As part of the AP-BT policy, among other things, the companies would enjoy a lower sales tax of just one per cent, down from the present 8 to 16 per cent, on all high-end biotechnology products produced within the State. They would also be able to book space at concessional rates at the proposed 600 square kilometre Genome Valley. The policy proposes setting up an exclusive Rs. 500 million venture capital fund. The policy also speaks of funding the biotechnology start-ups through the existing APIDC Venture Capital Ltd. The aim of the policy is to leverage on the existing strengths of the State for rapid commercialisation of biotechnology so that innovative biotechnology products and services could be produced in the State. AP has already numerous centres of excellence in healthcare, agriculture, and biotechnology. Its capital Hyderabad has earned an image of being the pharmaceutical and science capital of the country. The government is also trying to use its strength in the IT for the growth of bioinformatics in the State. For the rapid growth of this sector, the government has identified field diagnostics, therapeutics, pharmacogenomics, bioinformatics, agriculture, marine, industrial biotechnology and contract research as some of the thrust areas.

ICICI has planned a Knowledge Park at Turkapally near Hyderabad, for promotion of Life Sciences. Thus far, Rs. 310

million have been invested in the Knowledge Park, developed on a 200-acre site. It is a joint initiative of ICICI and the Andhra Pradesh Government. The ICICI Knowledge Park and the Biotechnology Park together form part of a larger blueprint of the Genome Valley project, which the Government plans to develop on a 600 sq. km area encompassing Medchal, Shameerpet, Kesara mandals in Rangareddi district and Uppal-Tarnaka corridor.

ICICI has signed an MOU with the Indian Institute of Chemical Technology (IJCT), Centre for Cellular and Molecular Biology (CCMB) and the University of Hyderabad, in a new 'knowledge network initiative'. This project has also been assisted by the Department of Scientific and Industrial Research (DSIR), to the tune of Rs. 15 million to set up a Virtual Information Project taken up by the Knowledge Park. The Park has been licensed under Section 25 of the Companies Act, 1956, and is approved by the Department of Scientific and Industrial Research, Government of India for the benefit of Customs duty exemption and Excise duty waiver. Under the initiative, partners in the Knowledge Park will get on-line access to library-based information expertise from these national labs and university system. It would also encourage undertaking collaborative research between corporates and research companies based in the park. The park has identified another 20 premier research organisations and universities during the first phase of the programme. At this point, only two start-ups—Medicorp Technologies and Pulsar Electro-Optics Ltd., have moved into the park with their projects. Two more companies are actively considering to move in. They are Bijam Biosciences Ltd., a Nagarjuna Group company which wants to set up a research centre in agri-biotech and MedGene Biotech, which plans to start a research centre for new drug discovery and genomics research.

Karnataka

The Karnataka Government has announced a biotechnology policy to promote this sector and is setting up an institute for bioinformatics in Bangalore. The Government is also creating a biotechnology fund which will have inflows from biotechnology companies.

This would be used for incubation of new projects and promotion of the sector in the State. The policy statement spells this out as an attempt to tap on the synergy between information technology and biotechnology as IT can immensely help in biotechnology research to achieve results faster.

The Karnataka Government is putting in Rs. 50 million and an equal amount is being brought in by ICICI to develop the Institute of Bioinformatics and Applied Biotechnology in Bangalore. The institute has four primary objectives: (i) conducting research in biotechnology, (ii) providing education and training in similar areas; (iii) providing incubation facilities for start-up projects with common facilities and (iv) creating a platform for educationist, scientists, industry, venture funds and Government, to interact with each other for the development of this sector in India.

Karnataka has planned to launch India's first state-sponsored biotechnology venture capital fund to boost their initiatives. The fund is likely to have an initial seed capital of Rs. 100 million to be operated through Karnataka State Industrial Investment and Development Corporation (KSIIDC)-Karnataka State Finance Corporation (KSFC). Karnataka was also the frontrunner in setting up the first state financed IT VC fund. It now proposes to extend Bangalore's numerous position in IT to other knowledge-based industries by floating a fund to support subjects like biotechnology, genetic engineering and pharmaceuticals. To supplement the modest initial contribution, the state has plans to mobilize additional funds for the biotechnology corpus from other domestic and global FIs and multilateral agencies. Recently, Karnataka's IT and commerce-industries team tried to pitch for a share in the \$ 1.2 billion incubation fund of Singapore's National Science and Technology Board (NSTB).

The Karnataka officials scoured for opportunities for financial, technical and marketing assistance for biotechnology ventures, besides aiming for joint R&D between Institute of Bioinformatics in Bangalore and Centre for Cellular and Molecular Biology, Hyderabad, and two top Singapore agencies, namely Institute of Molecular & Cellular Biology (IMCB) and Institute of Agribiology (IAB). Incidentally, as part of the biotechnology buildup. The Karnataka government is also setting up an ultra-modern Centre for Human Genetics at the Agriculture University campus in Bangalore over a 20-acre plot. It has also engaged Arthur Andersen to prepare a biotechnology strategy paper spelling out the infrastructure and policy framework required to boost its growth and to extract optimum advantage from this stream of new business.

Tamil Nadu

The Tamil Nadu Industrial Development Corporation (TIDCO) has linked a technical service agreement with Cornell University, USA for setting up a biotechnology park in Chennai, christened TICEL (Tidco Centre for Life Sciences), the park proposes to attract fresh investment of Rs.10,000 million from 50 new companies to be set up in the park and fuel bio-entrepreneurship. Among the states, Tamil Nadu is the only state, with such kind of foreign collaboration.

TICEL is modelled on the TIDRL Park, the information technology park set up by TIDCO, as per the MoU, valid for five years renewable for another five years; Cornell University will help from the conceptual stage to the commissioning stage of the park. The state-of-the-art park will provide complete technical and other allied services under one umbrella including technology transfer, monitoring, networking, contract and collaborative research work, product validation, documentation, commercialization, training and a separate intellectual property rights (IPR) cell which will support in the areas of patents, licensing royalty sharing and copyrights. The total cost is pegged at Rs. 625 million. TIDCO will be investing Rs. 90 million as equity. The Tamil Nadu government would bring in Rs. 200 million, while the remaining Rs. 330 million would be raised from various banks and financial institutions. It is stated that State Bank of India, Industrial Development Finance Corporation and Exim Bank have also shown interest in picking up equity state. The financial closure of the park is over in November 2001, and the park would be made ready for occupation by December 2002.

Cornell University in addition to the above, will also be setting up a special project cell at its premises in the USA to provide for advanced training, apart from offering access to its electronic library. It will also facilitate relationships between the tenants of similar parks abroad and in the Chennai park besides exchange of faculty for conducting specific and advanced training programmes. TICEL would be set up in a five-acre expense consisting of two major facilities—a bio-resource centre of 18,000 sq. ft. and customized laboratories of 1.2 lakh sq. ft. It will explore the Indian genetic pool and exploit the germplasm base available and leverage on the existing pool of Indian biotechnology scientists and low cost software skills.

Himachal Pradesh (HP)

Himachal Pradesh probably is the only Northern Indian state which has prepared a blue print for promotion of biotechnology industries in the State. This would include setting up of a biotechnology park at Solan, conservation and exploitation of bioresources, intensification of R&D, and promoting biotechnology entrepreneurship through tax concessions and relaxed labour laws. At Solan, land has been earmarked at New Solan to set up the biotech industries. The idea is to tap the huge potential of bio-resources and commercially exploit the state's rare herbal medicines, annual global trade flow of which is close to $ 20 billion. HP could help enhance the country's share as 3,295 plant species were present in the state. It is also proposed to provide research based support to the private companies in form of providing for instance, access to a database of bio resources which is being developed along with separate entries of endangered medicinal plants. Apart from this a germ plasm collection and culture facilities and bioinformatics network is also being established.

In order to tap these strengths, a series of concessions and sops have been chalked out. The industry has been given priority sector status and assured uninterrupted power supply at industrial rates. Labour laws have been relaxed, arrangements made for single window clearance of projects, with mega project status for ones with over Rs. 500 million investment. This would encourage diversification of farming through companies which are already into micro-propagation units in other states for plants and crops like ginger, saffron, potato, strawberry and bamboo.

Concluding Remarks

Over the years India has developed strengths in biotechnology in public sector institutions. 'In-graduation from Biotechnology Development Board to Department of Biotechnology in late eighties was a decisive step to address a wider canvas in biotechnology. In these years DBT has emerged as a major force to direct biotechnology developments in India. Further, the involvement of various agencies dealing with this technology has further helped in developing technology capability at various levels. The size of the industry is estimated to have grown to $ 1.5 to $ 2.5 billion between 1999 and 2002.There are two major research centres in India working on stem cell line research.

The achievements in biotechnology in India could become possible only because the government took early initiatives for setting up institutional infrastructure for human resource development. As of now more than 62 universities and institutions are engaged in biotechnology training and education related programmes. Efforts are being made to link up human resource development programmes according to industry requirements, and in fact, academic institutions are also being encouraged to work in close tandem with industry, India has attached greater importance to bioinformatics. DBT has set up 55 centres for bioinformatics, which have been developed as a strong information network. They are linked with databases and networks around the world. The whole range of new initiatives to support biotechnology programmes at Indian Institute of Technology and at Jawaharlal Nehru University are aimed in that direction. The micro propagation technology parks at TERI, New Delhi and NCL, Pune have served as an important interface between the industry and the developers of the technology in the areas of plant tissue culture. National

Centre for Plant Genome Research and National Brain Research Centre are some of the recent additions. However, it is difficult to estimate precise R&D allocations at several of these centres. The budgets of major funding agencies like CSIR/ICMR and ICAR give only an aggregate picture. Therefore, there is an urgent need to launch a detailed survey to collect specific biotechnology related allocations at the individual institute/laboratory level. Apart from this, DBT or some other such agency should urgently initiate an exercise for data collection either on its own or through specialised sectoral agencies.

These initiatives coupled with other industrial promotion efforts may encourage industry also to participate in this technology evolution exercise. Despite phenomenal growth and rapid penetration of this technology. However, the local firms are facing an intense competition from a whole range of transnational corporations. The pressure is immensely acute in the agricultural sector where Indian firms are finding it difficult to access relevant gene sequences given the proprietary rights of TNCs as developers of these technologies. In the pharmaceuticals sector, where advanced forms of biotechnology are being used, firms are facing severe liquidity constraints for investment. According to Ernst & Young, technology funding required for Indian biotechnology sector in 2001 was $ 2.5 billion while by 2010 it would be $ 4.8 billion. A larger part of this funding is for supporting development of an idea and also for diversification of activities of Indian firms.

2

POLICY ON EDUCATIONAL INFRASTRUCTURE FOR BIOTECHNOLOGY IN INDIA

The purpose of this chapter is to discuss educational infrastructure for science and technology (S&T) in India with special reference to Andhra Pradesh, biotechnology policy of the Government of India and the Government of Andhra Pradesh and the need for Human Resource Development for the growth of biotechnology.

Educational Infrastructure for S&T in India

Science and Technology has contributed a lot in improving the quality of life in all parts of the world and there are great expectations from Scientific and Technological developments within the country. The Government of India has attached considerable importance to science and technology and has created an impressive infrastructure over the years. This includes national laboratories, R&D institutions, academic institutions and industrial R&D units.

Starting from the early 1970s, there has been a significant increase in the Government support for science and technology. India today has a wide base of infrastructure for R&D. There are 200 universities, about 400 national laboratories and 1300 inhouse R&D units of industries (Ninth Five Year Plan 1997-2002, Planning Commission, New Delhi, 2001). As a result of this and other endowments, India has become internationally competitive in a number of areas. This progress has to be maintained and improved upon through appropriate training of manpower in the emerging technologies with infrastructural developments as the basic input and earmarking of funds for higher education by the scientific departments the form of direct support to identified centres in the universities.

The problems in bringing about improvements in S&T education pertain to the unavoidable socio-political influences on education, besides inadequacy of laboratory facilities in universities for research and teaching work at post-graduate and doctorate levels. The academic community has to engage itself in infrastructure building for higher education.

S&T in Andhra Pradesh

The Eighth Plan outlay for S&T for Andhra Pradesh (AP) was Rs. 200 lakhs. The years 1992-93, 1993-94, 1994-95 and 1995-96 registered Actuals of Rs. 13 lakhs, Rs. 15 lakhs, Rs. 10 lakhs, Rs. 20 lakhs and Rs. 56 lakhs respectively. Investment in biotechnology has been limited to few areas such as genetic engineering of microbes, plant tissue culture, enzyme technology, DNA finger printing, assisted reproduction technologies and rational drug design. Investment has just begun in the area of bioinformatics, which is a relatively new area devoted to analysis of the extremely large amount of information about biological systems and their constituents (such as DNA and Proteins) that is becoming available on an exponentially increasing scale for human good such as intelligent development of new drugs and of individual medicine. Bioinformatics requires a dual knowledge of modern biology and IT and is poised to give a new face to the latter.

India has enormous advantage in comparison to other countries for development of biotechnology—the right temperature, an amazing biodiversity, technical competence, an extensive scientific infrastructure, outstanding institutions in related areas, relatively inexpensive workforce, a dependable software industry and a flourishing drug industry. All these advantages are obtained in our state and to top it. Hyderabad is fast emerging as an intellectual and medical capital of India. The Biotechnology Policy Paper 2001 recently released by the Department of Industries and Commerce, Government of Andhra Pradesh, visualises a critical role for biotechnology in accelerating the pace of economic and social development of the State. The government has identified various sectors such as agriculture, medical and health, forestry, animal husbandry, environment protection and improvement in quality of products and services where biotechnology would be immensely beneficial.

The Government of Andhra Pradesh intends to facilitate the development of biotechnology in the State by creating high quality infrastructure through strategy of setting up specialised Biotech Parks in different parts of the State, encouraging research activities, developing human resources and establishing links between research institutions, academia and industry.

Existing Information Sources

Efforts in the direction of taking stock of R&D efforts were initiated at the national level well back since 1947. A Scheme on national register for scientific and technical infrastructure was introduced but it proved to be a time consuming and costly exercise. It was, therefore, decided to take up this activity along with the census survey.

The first survey of S&T infrastructure was conducted along with 1961 census of decennial population in which particulars of 2.45 lakh personnel were collected. Thereafter S&T surveys have been undertaken in 1971, 1981 and 1991 with variations in methodologies. Recent information sources include Government of Andhra Pradesh Policy Document on Biotechnology, 2001, E&Y Report—Beyond Borders, other published and unpublished literature, books, journals and working papers.

Biotechnology Policy in India—Government of India Policy

The setting up of a separate Department of Biotechnology (DBT), under the Ministry of Science and Technology in 1986 gave a new impetus to the development of the field of modern biology and biotechnology in India. In more than a decade of its existence, the department has promoted and accelerated the pace of development of biotechnology in the country. Through several R&D projects, demonstrations and creation of infrastructural facilities a clear visible impact of this field has been seen. The department has made significant achievements in the growth and application of biotechnology in the broad areas of agriculture, health care, animal sciences, environment and industry.

The impact of the biotechnology related developments in agriculture, health care, environment and industry, has already been visible and the efforts are now culminating into products and processes. More than 5000 research publications, 4000 post-doctoral students, several technologies transferred to industries and patents filed including US patents, can be considered as a modest beginning. Department of Biotechnology (DBT) has been interacting with more than 5,000 scientists per year in order to utilise the existing expertise of the universities and other national laboratories. A very strong peer reviewing and monitoring mechanism has been developed. There has been close interaction with the State Governments particularly through State S&T Councils for developing biotechnology application projects, demonstration of proven technologies, and training of human resource in States and Union Territories. Programmes with the states of Gujarat, Rajasthan, Madhya Pradesh, Orissa, West Bengal, Haryana, Punjab, Jammu & Kashmir, Mizoram, Andhra Pradesh and Uttar Pradesh have been evolved. Biotechnology Application Centres in Madhya Pradesh and West Bengal have already been started.

In India, more than a decade of concerted effort in research and development in identified areas of modern biology and biotechnology have given rich dividends. The proven technologies at the laboratory level have been scaled up and demonstrated in field. Patenting of innovations, technology transfer to industries and close interaction with them have given a new direction to biotechnology research. Initiatives have been taken to promote transgenic research in plants with emphasis on pest and disease resistance, nutritional quality, silk-worm genome analysis, molecular biology of human genetic disorders, brain research, plant genome research, development, validation and commercialisation of diagnostic kits and vaccines for communicable diseases, food biotechnology, biodiversity conservation and bioprospecting, setting up of micropropagation parks and biotechnology based development for SC/ST, rural areas, women and for different States.

The DBT was established in 1986 with the following mandate:

- Support R&D and manufacturing in Biology
- Identify and set up Centres of Excellence for R&D
- Promote large scale use of Biotechnology
- Integrated Programme for Human Resource Development
- Establishment of Infrastructure
- Facilities to support R&D and production
- Serve as nodal point for the collection and dissemination of information relating to biotechnology
- Promote University and Industry Interaction
- Evolve Bio Safety Guidelines
- To serve as Nodal Point for specific International Collaborations
- Manufacture and application of cell based vaccines
- Responsibility for Autonomous Institutions

The Department of Biotechnology considers financial support for grants-in-aid to various R&D institutions and Universities for Research and Development activities in Biotechnology. The broad categories under which programmes and projects are supported by this department are discussed in this section.

- Research and Development
- Biotech Product, Process Development, Technology Transfer
- Human Resource Development
- Centres of Excellence
- Biotechnology Information System (BTIS)
- International Collaboration
- Jai Vigyan National S&T Missions
- National Bioresource Board
- New Patent Cell

The DBT's vision for Biotechnology research, development and commercialisation, in the next 10 years, focuses on:

- Basic Research in New Biology and Biotechnology
  (a) Genomics
  (b) Bioinformatics
  (c) Basic biological phenomena with potential application
- Agriculture, Plant and Animal Biotechnology
- Environment and Biodiversity
- Medical Biotechnology
- Biofuels
- Bioprocesses, Product Development, and Bioinstrumentation
- Human Resource Development
- Creation and Strengthening of Infrastructure in Existing Institutions and setting up new Institutions
- Biotechnology for Societal Development
- Biosafety, Ethical and Proprietary Issues

Infrastructure and Institution Development

- Biotechnology parks, repositories, hardening units, genome sequencing facilities, new centres of excellence as per the need to be created.
- Strengthening of existing infrastructure facilities with expansion wherever necessary.
- Creation of centres of excellence in frontier areas in existing institutions, and where necessary, start new centres in carefully chosen frontier areas.
- Infrastructure for undertaking investigations in the frontier areas of research (Functional Genomics, Proteomics, Bioinformatics), containment facilities as required under biosafety regulations and exclusive units for dealing with intellectual property rights to be built.
- Setting up facilities for sequencing (DNA and Protein) on payment basis so that this routine yet necessary information could be retrieved without wasteful expenditure and

resource. This would go a long way in rapid characterization of the large diversity that will be added to the existing gene pool. This will also hasten the process of any species/genus descriptions since this too would not now be feasible without 16 sequence availability. Considering the expanse of the country and likely inventory of the gene pool, perhaps 6 sequencing facilities as a commercial venture would be required in next 2 years. In 10 years, 12-15 facilities with industry cooperation to be set up.

Human Resource Development

An integrated Human Resource Development Programme is being implemented to generate adequate and appropriately trained personnel in the area of Biotechnology. Sustained efforts in generating trained human resource has given rich dividends in bringing excellence in this field and providing the skilled human resource for research and industry. The various schemes are:

- Post-Graduate, Post-Doctoral and Post-M.D./M.S. Programme
- Biotechnology Associateships
- Training Programmes
- Visiting Scientist from Abroad Programme
- Golden Jubilee Biology Scholarships
- Golden Jubilee Biotechnology Fellowships
- Popularisation of Biotechnology
- Seminars/Symposia/Conferences

Post-Graduate, Post-Doctoral and Post-M.D./M.S. Programme

In order to meet the long-term requirement of trained personnel in the multidisciplinary field of biotechnology, post-graduate courses at M.Sc./M.V.Sc./M.Tech. level have been supported in selected universities/institutions. These courses at the number of places being run are:

Table 2.1 : Details of DBT Sponsored Courses

Sl. No.	*Name of the Course*	*Duration*	*No. of Universities/ Institutions*
1.	M.Sc. courses in general Biotechnology	2 yrs	23
2.	M.Sc. courses in Agricultural Biotechnology	2 yrs	7
3.	M.V.Sc. course in Neurosciences	3 yrs	1
4.	M.Sc. course in Medical Biotechnology	2 yrs	1
5.	M.Sc. course in Marine Biotechnology	2 yrs	1
6.	M.Tech/M.Sc.(Tech.) in Biochemical Engineering, Bioprocess Technology and Biotechnology	3 sem/ 5 yrs integrated	4
7.	PG Diploma in Medical Biotechnology & Biochemical Engineering	1 yr	2
8.	Post MD/MS Certificate/Training Course	1 yr	31

Source: DBT Website

The total intake of students to these courses is around 500 per year. Students are taught subjects like cell biology, molecular biology, genetic engineering, immunology, tissue culture, biochemical engineering and bioprocess technology, computer modelling of molecular structures and interactions, bioinformatics, marine biology etc. The current topics such as IPR, biosafety and ethical issues have also been included in the curriculum. Students are sent for training in industries and research institutions during summer vacations for a period of 4-6 weeks.

Biotechnology Associateships

This programme provides the scientists employed in academic and research institutions and actively engaged in research in the field of biotechnology, an opportunity for pursuing advanced research and to undergo specialised training within and outside the country. Two types of associateships, namely national and overseas are awarded.

National Associateship

The national associateship is awarded to carry advanced research in leading Indian research institutions for a period of 9 months to 2 years under a Supervisor other than the candidate's parent institution. The scheme also has a provision for training in an overseas laboratory for a period of 3 months provided one complete 9 months of associateship in India successfully and the overseas component of the training is justifiable.

Overseas Associateship

These awards are made under two categories, namely *long-term* and *short-term*. The long-term associateship is tenable for one year whereas the short-term is awarded for 3 to 6 months. On an average 25 scientists are selected for both long-term and short-term awards.

Training Programmes

Short-term Training Courses for Mid-Career Scientists

These courses are conducted by universities/research institutions having adequate facilities and expertise in the subject. The participants are mainly mid-career scientists from academic and research institutions and also from industrial R&D laboratories. The course is conducted for a period of 15 days to one month and the number of participants are usually 12-15. The courses lay emphasis on practical training in modern and advanced laboratory techniques and also in emerging areas of biotechnology. It provides opportunity to scientists to acquire expertise in the modern areas of biotechnology and therefore helps them in their research activities. Some of the areas in which the courses are conducted include molecular biology and related emerging areas, taxonomy, industrial biotechnology, immunology, plant tissue culture and marine/agriculture biotechnology.

Technician Training

Keeping in view the utility and requirement of trained technicians for various biotechnological research and development activities in the country, short-term (2 to 3 months duration) and long-term (1 year duration). Technician training programmes are being supported by the Department.

Post-M.Sc. and M.Tech. Training in Industries:

- As industries prefer persons with some exposure to industrial operations for jobs, the students passing out the M.Sc./M.Tech courses are selected for training in biotech based industries for a period of six months. Such a training would enhance the career opportunities of students in industries.
- To orient biotechnology post-graduates to the needs of the biotech industry, Biotech Consortium India Limited (BCIL), a company promoted by the department, is implementing this training programme on behalf of the department.

Visiting Scientist from Abroad Programme

The objective of the programme is to gain and share the current state of knowledge in the frontier areas of Biotechnology through visits of experts from technologically advanced countries to the research institutions/universities in India, which are engaged in modern biotechnological research activities. The visiting Scientists participate in collaborative research programmes or in training activities at premier R&D institutions and universities in India.

Golden Jubilee Biology Scholarship

On the occasion of the celebration of India's 50 years independence, the golden jubilee biology scholarship scheme was introduced in place of the earliest scheme of DBT scholarships in biology. These scholarships are given to students from among the top 40 rank holders in biology at the CBSE +2 level examination. Only those students who continue their studies in biology or related subject at the undergraduate level are eligible for the scholarship as the aim of the scheme is to encourage brilliant students to continue biology study.

Golden Jubilee Biotechnology Fellowships

As part of the Golden Jubilee celebration of India's independence the department has introduced a scheme to award—

- One golden jubilee biotechnology senior fellowship and
- Two golden jubilee biotechnology fellowships.

The senior fellowship carries a cash award of Rs.1 lakh plus a contingency grant of Rs. 50,000, whereas the other category of the fellowship carries a cash award of Rs.50,000 plus a contingency grant of Rs. 30,000. These awards are given to scientists who have made outstanding contributions in the field of modern biology and biotechnology in the country.

Popularisation of Biotechnology

Biotechnology Publications

The programme is being implemented through the National Institute of Science Communication (NISCOM), CSIR, New Delhi. The objectives of the programme are to create awareness about basic concepts, potentials and recent developments in biotechnology, among the students and general public. Out of the 10 popular monographs published earlier in English, 3 have already been translated in Hindi for the benefit of students and general public in Hindi speaking region, about 10 colour posters on various Biotechnological processes have been brought out. An illustrated dictionary of biotechnology is being compiled. Popular articles are being published regularly under the Biotechnology column in *Science Reporter* and *Vigyan Pragati.* A popular monograph for hildren has also been published. More such publications are rought out from time to time.

'opular Lectures by Experts

Jnder this programme, a series of popular lectures by experts are rganised by academic/research institutions engaged in iotechnology research activities in order to create awareness mong school/college/university students, and teachers as well as eneral public about the recent developments in biotechnology nd its potential applications.

Vational Science Day

'he department provides financial assistance to a number of istitutions which are conducting DBT sponsored Post-Graduate 'rogrammes in Biotechnology to celebrate the National Science)ay every year. During the celebrations various activities like)pen-houses, exhibitions and debates, essay competitions, quiz rogrammes etc. on various subjects of biotechnology are onducted by the institutions. The celebrations are also attended y students of nearby schools and colleges and also general ublic.

eminars/Symposia/Conferences

Inder this scheme partial or full financial assistance is given to ducational and research institutions, registered societies etc. for rganising national and international seminars/symposia/conferen-es on topics in biotechnological related areas, which provide pportunity to our leading scientists and young research workers) discuss issues related to research in the area of biotechnology 'ith their counterparts working in the country or abroad.

'entres of Excellence, Repositories and Biotech Facilities

iteraction with Industry, services and supplies, in-house R&D

and database development have been the major activities of all the facilities in the respective areas of specialization. The division is divided into three subdivisions:

- Repositories
- Programme Support and Centres for Excellence
- Biotech Facilities

Repositories

Main objectives of this scheme is to promote establishment o repositories for conservation of living organisms includin microbes both useful and harmful in agriculture, human health animal husbandry and bio-industry. These repositories may als serve as referral centres. Various repositories established unde this scheme are:

- Microbial Type Culture Collection (MTCC) at IMTECH Chandigarh.
- National Facilities for Conservation and Utilisation o Blue Green Algae (BGAC), IARI, New Delhi.
- National Facility for Marine Cynobacterial Germ Plasm Collection (NFMC), Bharathidasan University, Tiruchira palli.
- National Facility for Plant Tissue Culture Repositor (NFPTCR), NBPGR, New Delhi.
- Repository on Filarial Parasites and Reagents at MGIMS Sevargram, Wardha.
- Repository on Medicinal and Aromatic Plant Materials a CIMAP, Lucknow.
- Repository on Cryopreservation of blood cells at India Institute of Hematology, Mumbai.

Programme Support and Centres for Excellence

Under this scheme support is provided for establishment o programme based centres, facilities and centres for excellence various areas of advanced biotechnology and modern biolog

Such centres undertake basic research in modern biology leading to specific products and processes through a team work and also serve as major infrastructure facility extending services to the scientific community.

Programme support provided under this scheme includes—

- High priority areas of Biology, IISC, Bangalore
- Cellular control processes and molecular genetics of biotic and abiotic stress of plants, CCMB, Hyderabad
- Biotechnology projects to Rajiv Gandhi Centre for Biotechnology, Thiruvananthapuram
- New Initiatives for North-East Region, Bioresources Development Centre

Biotechnology Information System (BTIS)—A National Bioinformatics Network

India was the first country that had taken giant step in 1986 and established a nationwide Bioniformation System of India. The Department of Biotechnology (DBT) had taken this major leap forward after carrying out both micro and macro level planning with a mission to make India a leader in Bioinformatics. The Biotechnology Information System (BTIS) Programme of Department of Biotechnology was launched during the Seventh Five Year Plan to harness the scientific knowledge in various inter-disciplinary areas of biotechnology.

The programme is comprised of a distributed database and network system, namely Biotechnology Information System Network (BTISnet). Under the BTISnet, the Distributed Centres were located in those cities and institutes where active research work in the area of Biotechnology was in progress. In the second phase, several subcentres were established in various Universities and Research Institutes who were running major biotechnology programmes and projects. As a consequence of this initiative, computer literacy and awareness among Bio-scientists has grown significantly. Large number of public domain databases with regular updates, in the area of molecular biology and genetic engineering have become available to scientists of India. Computer hardware to carry out simple data analysis and modelling is also available through this programme. NICNET provided the initial connectivity to all these centres through V-SAT. Internet connection became available through NICNET, ERNET and VSNL making the Bioinformatics centres and sub-centres hub of activities related to data access, data analysis and modelling. Major databanks, such as Animal Virus Information System, of International Standard, have been developed in the country. Software tools for sequence analysis on work stations were developed in the country in the form of software packages and made available at a low cost to various universities, colleges and research institutes. India became a node of the Microbial Strain Data Network, Hybridoma Data Bank and EMBnet as well as Asian Pacific Countries Bioinformatics Network. Under the FARM programme, India was chosen to be nodal country to provide training and coordination of the Information network for Agricultural scientists in eight countries belonging to South East Asia. Shortage of manpower in this new area has been tackled by conducting a large number of short-term courses and long-term courses at four selected centres—University of Pune, Madurai Kamraj University, Calcutta University, and Jawaharlal Nehru University.

DBT with the help of NIC is updating connectivity by providing V-SATs of 64/128 KBPS bandwidth to selected centres. The network has established links among scientists in organizations involved in R&D and manufacturing activities in Biotechnology. Since its establishment, the BTISnet is providing a single major information resource in the country covering several inter-disciplinary areas of biotechnology including molecular biology data, bibliographic information and management information covering R&D projects and profile of research activities in the country. The network has also established linkages with various national and international information networks through the modern computer and communication systems by implementing several network services such as e-mail, discussion groups on the Internet and other Internet based facilities for access to worldwide resources in biotechnology.

Andhra Pradesh Scenario

The Government of Andhra Pradesh Biotechnology Policy Paper 2001, highlights the existing network of research laboratories, such as the Centre for Cellular and Molecular Biology (CCMB), Centre for DNA Fingerprinting and Diagnostics (CDFD), Indian Institute of Chemical Technology (IICT), International Crop Research Institute for Arid and Semi-Arid Tropics (ICRISAT), the Directorate of Rice Research (DRR), and other specialised agro-research centres of the Indian Council of Agricultural Research (ICAR), Indian Agricultural Rural Institute (IARI), National Academy of Agricultural Research Management (NAARM), National Institute of Nutrition (NIN), Dr. Reddy's Research Foundation (DRF), Aurobindo Research Centre, ICICI Knowledge Park Ltd., Hyderabad Eye Research Foundation, Institute of Genetics and Hospital for Genetic Diseases and the Life Sciences Departments of the University of Hyderabad and of Osmania University. This infrastructure for research is expected to provide the necessary support to the development of biotechnology in the State. Specialised institutions such as the Centre for Cellular and Molecular Biology (CCMB), have been identified as "Centres for Excellence" in biotechnology.

In addition, the Policy paper highlights on the existing pool of scientific and technical manpower. Andhra Pradesh has 9 universities located in different parts of the State, viz., Osmania University, Jawharlal Nehru Technological University, Acharya N.G. Ranga Agricultural University, Kakatiya University, Nagarjuna University, Andhra University, Sri Venkateswara University, Sri Krishna Devaraya University and Sri Padmavati Mahila Visvavidyalayam which offer undergraduate and post-graduate level courses in biotechnology at present. Some of them are sponsored by the Department of Science and Technology, Government of India (Annexure-A). According to the Policy document, about 900 students at the graduate level and 200 students at the post-graduate level pass out of these institutions. In addition, the University of Hyderabad, Acharya N.G. Ranga Agricultural University, Medical Institutes such as NIMS and SVIMS, the

NTR Health University and their centres have R&D facilities in various areas of biotechnology.

The Policy document also indicates the intention of the Government of Andhra Pradesh to provide high quality infrastructure at reasonable cost with integrated services to biotech manufacturing units by setting up a series of Biotech Parks throughout the State. The physical infrastructure envisaged include piped water supply, electricity substation, telecommunications, with fibre optic connectivity, and approach road. A National Resource Centre is also envisaged which will provide common facilities to the biotech companies, incubators, specialized animal house facilities for laboratory experimentation, breeding of experimental animal models etc. There is also mention of a critical mass existing in Andhra Pradesh for the Biotech Industry. The presence of several pioneers—host of public and private enterprises in the field of biotechnology, and presence of talented entrepreneurs is also highlighted.

To sum up, the human resource development would determine the success or otherwise of the biotechnology advances. Not only the policy framework has to be adequate but its implementation and the focus have also to be appropriate to enable the biotechnology advances yield the desired results. The requisite human resource development alone could ensure a resounding success on each of these parameters.

3

MULTI-DIMENSIONAL ANALYSIS OF EDUCATIONAL INFRASTRUCTURE VIS-À-VIS THE BIOTECH SECTOR

This chapter outlines the various dimensions related to educational infrastructure in biotechnology, and the SWOT (Strengths Weaknesses, Opportunities and Threats) analysis pertaining to biotech sector in India.

The social awareness of technological developments and socio-economic utilities emerging from them takes place gradually. Apart from the gestation period involved in conceiving a technology product and its ultimate delivery, the users of the product take time to understand and appreciate its utility. As time is an important dimension in any technological development, it becomes necessary to ascertain that the entire process from product development to marketing is sustained and attempts are made to progress further. One of the main ingredients for a sustained technology/product development is creating an appropriate framework of scientific and technical infrastructure and institutions. Creating such a framework involves investment in both the physical and intellectual capital. In general, these may include, laboratories, scientific equipment, trained scientific and technical manpower, administrative support, industrial and institutional linkages, industry-training facilities, creating a stakeholder environment, venture capitalists, public investment, patents, IPRs, public policy issues such as regulation, and alignment of private initiatives with public vision. The significant roles of various quarters is quite visible in this framework.

Educational infrastructure forms an important component of

this framework. As 'infra' is to 'foundation underneath', the purpose of such an infrastructure is to support and maintain a balance in the 'demand' and 'supply' market for scientific and technical manpower. This chapter is an attempt to place in the above context, the existing scenario of educational infrastructure for biotechnology. The working paper aims to attract comments and suggestions from experts in the field of biotechnology.

Educational infrastructure for biotechnology includes:

—Scientific and technical experts in universities, scientific institutes and CSIR Institutes.

—Graduate and post-graduate students, doctoral and post-doctoral research scholars, project associates.

—Courses and curricula on biotechnology being offered in various universities and educational institutions; courses on bioinformatics—a backbone for databases and computational tools.

—Scientific and technical personnel in inhouse R&D establishments—public and private enterprises.

—Physical infrastructure existing in departmental labs in the universities, and R&D facilities in scientific institutions and CSIR Institutes.

Resources at macro level that support development of such an educational infrastructure may include:

—Access to genetic resources.

—Common platforms for information sharing and technology development—biotech parks.

Biotechnology in India

"India is on the threshold of a biotechnology revolution, which is set to be the new engine of growth for the economy. With the availability of a vast pool of scientific talent, presence of a world-class Information Technology (IT) industry and a vibrant generic pharmaceutical sector, India is very much on its way to emerge as a force to reckon with in the global biotech arena. The market for biotech products in India is at present valued at $ 2.5 billion, a five-fold increase since 1997. This is mainly because at present the biotech market focuses on low-end products like vaccines, not cutting-edge genomics or proteonomics. According to growth estimates by the Confederation of Indian Industries, over the next five years, biotechnology can offer opportunities for fresh investment of Rs. 7 billion to Rs.8 billion in India. This fresh investment, if realised, could result in a turnover of Rs.9 billion to Rs. 10 billion during the next 5 to 7 years." [N. Janardhana Rao, Biotech: India Inc.'s New Growth Engine, *Chartered Financial Analyst,* August 2002, p.24]

Dimensions for Study

1. Whether there is an increase in the capital expenditure for infrastructure development in the field of biotechnology?
2. Whether there is an increase in the number of courses offered in biotechnology and allied subjects?
3. What is the existing strength of post-doctoral and doctoral scholars, post-graduate and graduate students working in the field of biotechnology?
4. What is the existing strength of Scientific and Technical Personnel in this field?
5. Are there any training programmes, international conferences, symposia, etc. envisaged by the institutes/industry establishments for imparting training to researchers and personnel involved in biotechnology?
6. Are there any scholarships for students and researchers in biotechnology?
7. How does the industry contribute to the biotechnology education—does it sponsor any project/provide scholarships?
8. Are there any extension programmes/awareness programmes?
9. What is the existing physical infrastructure—including labs and major scientific equipment, access to databases?
10. Are the courses on biotechnology offered at graduate and post-graduate level theoretical or application oriented?

11. What is the perception of the Industry to the courses and curricula on biotechnology?
12. What is the placement record for various courses in biotechnology?

There may be possibility of identifying some interdependency within these broad aspects, which would be accorded due importance while analysing the inputs and coming out with the findings.

SWOT Analysis of Indian Biotech Sector

Strengths

- Trained manpower and knowledge base
- Good network of research laboratories
- Rich Bio-diversity
- Well developed base industries (e.g., pharmaceuticals, seeds)
- Access to intellectual resources of NRIs in this area
- Extensive clinical trials and research—access to vast and diverse disease populations
- Bio-diversity—India's human gene pools offer an exciting opportunity for genomic research. Unique and diverse plant, animal and microbial bio-diversity also provides exciting research opportunities

Weaknesses

- Missing link between research and commercialization
- Lack of venture capital
- Relatively low R&D expenditure by industry
- Image of Indian industry—doubts about ability of Indian companies to develop original products for international markets

Opportunities

- Large market
- Export potential
- Base for contract research for international companies due to rising costs of R&D abroad
- Large number of patients covering wider range of diseases—clinical research/trials

Threats

- Danger of anti-biotech propaganda gaining ground
- IPR policies

Source: Kiran Mazumdar Shaw, Biotechnology: Emerging Opportunities, *Chartered Financial Analyst,* August 2002, p.33.

To sum up, the dimensions of educational infrastructure for biotechnology are variegated and require a multi-pronged approach for their fuller comprehension in the absence of which it would not be possible to formulate appropriate paradigms to provide competitive edge to biotechnology industry in India.

4

TRENDS IN BIOTECHNOLOGY EDUCATION AND TRAINING

This chapter presents an analysis of the infrastructure for biotechnology education in India.

Post-graduate and Post-doctoral Programmes

A model system of Post-Graduate and Post-Doctoral teaching in biotechnology has been evolved. Table 4.1 gives the list of leading universities/institutions sponsored by DBT all over the country offering courses on biotechnology education. These universities/ institutions have been selected on the basis of expertise and infrastructure facilities available in the institute, the major on going R&D programmes in related areas, grants received from other funding agencies and nearness of other institutes/national laboratories engaged in biotechnology research. The Department has played a catalytic role by establishing these model institutes and this has stimulated several other institutes/universities to establish such institutional facilities on their own. Top grade students with background in basic and applied biology, chemistry, physics etc. are selected on All India basis and all selected students are given studentship. Krishnaswamy Committee on Integrated Manpower Planning, which submitted its report in 1988, has recommended continuation of the programmes and also introduction of some new institutions conducting post-graduate programmes in biotechnology.

Table 4.1 : DBT Sponsored Universities/Institutions offering Regular Teaching & Training Courses in Biotechnology in India: *As on 01-04-2004*

Sl. No.	*Name of the Institute/University*	*Annual Intake*
	M.Sc. General Biotechnology (2-year Courses)	
1.	Jawaharlal Nehru University, New Delhi (1985-86)	30
2.	Madurai Kamaraj University, Madurai (1985-86)	25
3.	MS University, Baroda (1985-86)	25
4.	University of Poona, Pune (1985-86)	20
5.	Banaras Hindu University, Varanasi (1986-87)	12
6.	Indian Institute of Technology, Mumbai (1987-88)	16
7.	Indian Instt. of Technology, Roorkee (1991-92) (formerly Roorkee University)	24
8.	Aligarh Muslim University, Aligarh (1991-92)	14
9.	Guru Nanak Dev University, Amritsar (1991-92)	10
10.	Devi Ahilya Viswavidyalaya, Indore (1991-92)	10
11.	University of Hyderabad, Hyderabad (1991-92)	10
12.	Himachal Pradesh University, Shimla (1994-95)	12
13.	University of Calicut, Kerala (1994-95)	12
14.	Banasthali Vidyapeeth, Banasthali, Rajasthan (1994-95) (For Girls Only)	25
15.	Tezpur University, Tezpur (Assam) (1998-99)	12
16.	Gulbarga University, Gulbarga (Karnataka) (1998-99)	10
17.	Jammu University, Jammu (1999-2000)	10
18.	Gujarat University, Ahmedabad (1999-2000)	10
19.	Mysore University, Mysore (1999-2000)	10
20.	University of Allahabad, Allahabad (1999-2000)	12
21.	Guru Jambheshwar University, Hisar (2000-2001)	14
22.	University of Kashmir, Srinagar (2000-2001)	10
23.	Kumaun University, Nainital (2000-2001)	10
24.	University of North Bengal, Siliguri (2001-2002)	10
25.	Lucknow University, Lucknow (2002-2003)	10
26.	Utkal University, Bhubneshwar (2002-2003)	10
27.	Pondicherry University, Pondicherry (2002-2003)	10
28.	Sri Padmavathi Mahila Visvavidyalayam, Thirupathi (2003-04)	10
29.	Nagpur University, Nagpur (2003-2004)	10
30.	Visva-Bharathi, Shantiniketan (WB) (2003-04)	10

(*contd.*)

(*contd.* **Table 4.1**)

Sl. No.	*Name of the Institute/University*	*Annual Intake*
	M.Sc. Agricultural Biotechnology (2 years)	
1.	Assam Agricultural University, Jorhat (1988-89)	10
2.	Tamil Nadu Agricultural University, Coimbatore (1988-89)	15
3.	GB Pant University of Agriculture and Technology, Pantnagar (1988-89)	20
4.	Himachal Pradesh Krishi Vishvavidhyalaya, Palampur (H.P.) (1999-2000)	05
5.	Indira Gandhi Agricultural University, Raipur (2000-2001)	10
6.	Marathwada Agricultural University, Parbhani (2000-2001)	10
7.	Orissa University of Agriculture & Technology, Bhubneshwar (2002-2003)	10
	Master in Medical Biotechnology (2 years)	
1.	All India Institute of Medical Sciences, New Delhi (1986-87)	10
	M.Sc. Marine Biotechnology (2 years)	
1.	Goa University, Goa (1988-89)	20
2.	Annamalai University, Parangipettai (2002-2003)	10
	M.Sc. Neurosciences (3/2 years)	
1.	Tata Institute of Fundamental Research, Mumbai (2000-2001) *(3 years)*	05
2.	Jiwaji University, Gwalior (2003-04)	10
3.	National Brain Research Centre, Gurgaon (2003-04)	10
	M.Sc. Industrial Biotechnology	
1.	Sardar Patel University, Vallabh Vidhyanagar (2003-04)	10

(*contd.*)

(*contd.* **Table 4.1**)

Sl. No.	*Name of the Institute/University*	*Annual Intake*
	M.Tech Biochemical Engineering & Biotechnology (5 years integrated /4 semesters/2 years course)	
1.	Indian Institute of Technology, Kharagpur (1986-87)	20
2.	Indian Institute of Technology, New Delhi (1986-87) Dual degree (5-year integrated as well as 4 semester courses) since 1993-94	10
3.	Anna University, Chennai (1991-92)	25
4.	University Institute of Chemical Technology, Mumbai (formerly UDCT, Mumbai) (1993-94)	30
5.	West Bengal University of Technology, Kolkata (2002-2003)	15
6.	Indian Institute of Technology, Kanpur (2002-2003)	10
	M.Tech. Pharmaceutical Biotechnology (2 years)	
1.	National Institute of Pharmaceutical Education & Research, Mohali (2003-04)	10
	Post MD/MS Certificate Course in Medical Biotechnology (1 year)	
1.	All India Institute of Medical Science, New Delhi	04
2.	Sanjay Gandhi Post Graduate Institute of Medical Sciences, Lucknow (2000-2001)	05
	PG Diploma Course in "Genetic Engineering & Bioprocess Development" (1 year)	
1.	M.S. University of Baroda, Baroda (2002-2003)	12
	PG Diploma Courses in Molecular & Biochemical Technology (1 year)	
1.	Sri Venkateshwara College (University of Delhi), New Delhi (1999-2000)	20

Source: DBT Website.

The post-graduate programmes are continuously being monitored by the Department through meetings of the Advisory Committees, meetings of the Course Coordinators and the National Board of Studies. Infrastructure facilities by way of equipment and laboratory have been built up in these institutes, which has influenced the teaching standards in these universities in the country.

Table 4.2 below explains about the number of admissions made each year to PG programmes in biotechnology from the year 1985-86 to 2000-2001.

Table 4.2 : The Number of Admissions to the PG Courses in BT from 1985-99 to 2000-2001

Sl. No.	*Year*	*Number of Admissions*
1.	1985-86	64
2.	1986-87	11
3.	1987-88	147
4.	1988-89	179
5.	1989-90	134
6.	1990-91	154
7.	1991-92	192
8.	1992-93	196
9.	1993-94	300
10.	1994-95	350
11.	1995-96	350
12.	1996-97	400
13.	1997-98	450
14.	1998-99	450
15.	1999-00	500
16.	2000-01	550

Post M.Sc. & M.Tech. Training in Industries

It has been found that many industries insist on some experience of working in industry for giving employment to students after post-graduation. It was, therefore, proposed to have a programme for training courses in Biotechnology sponsored by DBT which would be helpful to them in finding employment. Some may even get absorbed in the same industry. It may also help some trainees to start industries on their own.

Students passing out of the post-graduate courses in BT are selected and placed for training in various biotech based industries for period of 6 months. This scheme is being implemented through the Biotech Consortium India Ltd. (BCIL), New Delhi. Initially in a year around 25 students were selected for training in various industries in the country. The information from the year 1993-94 2001-02 is given in Table 4.3.

Table 4.3 : Number of Post-M.Sc. & M.Tech Students placed in Industrial Training from 1993-2002

Sl. No.	*Year*	*Number of students placed for training*
1.	1993-94	18
2.	1994-95	30
3.	1995-96	20
4.	1996-97	24
5.	1997-98	20
6.	1998-99	25
7.	1999-00	22
8.	2000-01	30
9.	2001-02	45

From the above Table 4.3, we can see that in the last 9 years an average of 27 persons have been placed in the industry for training. The highest number being trained in 2001-2002 with 45 students having got the training. Compared to the number of students who pass out of post-graduation, this number who get training is very small.

Technician Training Programmes

Well trained technicians are an asset to any good research laboratory. They play a vital role in research laboratories by making arrangements for/and performing standard/routine experiments as desired by senior scientists. This enables the scientists to devote their time more effectively for productive research. There is a dearth of technicians properly trained in modern laboratory techniques.

The Department of Biotechnology has formulated 2 types of Technician Training Scheme, viz., Short-term (3 months duration) and Long-term (1 to 2 years duration). Under the Short-term Technicians/Technical Assistants/Technologists in research laboratories are trained for a duration of 2 to 3 months in order to upgrade their skills.

Two long-term Technician Diploma Programmes each of one year's duration have been started with the financial support of OBT at Madurai Kamaraj University, Madurai and Sri Venkateswara College, University of Delhi, New Delhi. The former course started during 1989-90 and the latter started in the academic session of 1990-91. Number of admissions available in these courses during 1989-90 to 1998-99 is shown in Table 4.4.

Table 4.4 : Number of Admissions for Technician Training Programme 1990-1998

Sl. No.	*Year*	*Number of Admissions*
1.	1990-91	21
2.	1991-92	20
3.	1992-93	22
4.	1993-94	21
5.	1994-95	24
6.	1995-96	22
7.	1996-97	20
8.	1997-98	27

Short-term Training Programmes

The department sponsors a few short-term training courses (2-4 weeks duration) every year to impart practical training on newly emerging research techniques in areas of modern biotechnology. The objective of the programme is to provide practical hands-on training to mid-career scientists for meeting the requirements of newer R&D techniques in Biotechnology within the country. The department identifies areas of training as well as universities, national laboratories and other research institutions which have level of expertise and adequate infrastructure for organising such courses. Mid-career scientists/technologists engaged in research activities sponsored by their parent institutions are given preference for attending the courses with the idea that the participants on returning to their parent institutions could utilize techniques/ knowledge gained during the courses in their R&D teaching programmes the funds are provided for purchase of minor laboratory equipment/accessories, spares, consumables and other recurring expenses needed for organising the course. Provision has been made for inviting 3-4 guest faculty from within the country and if necessary one foreign expert also, in gap areas for each of the courses, so that the participants in each course get an opportunity to interact with the leading scientists working within as well as outside the country in particular research areas. From the year 1986 to 1998 about 70 institutions have conducted together about 185 short-term training programmes sponsored by DBT (Table 4.5).

Table 4.5 : Number of Short-Term Training Programmes during 1986-2000

Sl. No.	*Year*	*Number of Programmes*
1.	1986	9
2.	1987	12
3.	1988	11
4.	1989	14
5.	1990	14
6.	1991	16
7.	1992	11
8.	1993	14
9.	1994	12
10.	1995	13
11.	1996	13
12.	1997	9
13.	1998	14
14.	1999	11
15.	2000	8

Critical Examination

Through the above programmes we see that the three major approaches to capability building has been addressed, namely:

- Developing new talents in Biotechnology;
- Reorientation of exiting scientific manpower;
- Upgradation of the present BT manpower.

It could be seen that while PG courses in BT, technician training programmes and Post M.Sc., M.Tech Industrial training aim at the first category. Post-doc programmes, short-term training programmes come under the second and BT associateships promote upgradation of existing BT manpower developing new talents in Biotechnology.

The Post-Graduate courses in BT are very important for laying the foundation for the manpower in BT. The most important in this connection is the number of Universities which offer this programme and the number of seats they offer per year. It is seen that the number of Universities has increased from 11 in 1987 to 15 in 1990 and 22 in 1992 and 39 in 1998 and became 45 by 2001. The number of students admitted each year has followed a quadratic model as confirmed by the trend extrapolation model. We see that the Universities initially started at metropolitan cities, are now being started in relatively non-metropolitan cities also. The trend extrapolation indicates the need for either increasing the number of Universities, facilities and the very influencing interaction between the students passing out of these courses, in order to maintain the trend. The training in industries for the post-M.Sc. and M.Tech students is very important for aiding them to use their knowledge in their employment or to even start an industry of their own. Seeing that the present out-turn of students is around 500 per year, students selected for training in various industries is very small an average of only 27 students in the past 9 years have received the training and out of them only a few have secured jobs. So it indicates the need to increase the opportunities for industrial training. More number of industries may have to come forward to take the students for training, students for the benefit of the country.

In the present day, we see that technicians are preferred in the industries. So in that angle when we look into, it is important to train more number of technicians. But unfortunately only 2 institutions offer this solid training programme. So the out-turn of technicians is only 22 per year on an average. This indicates the necessity of giving more attention to expand this course in more number of institutions. The trend extrapolation shows that it is linear and hence even over the next 10 years hardly the number increases by 10. So this indicates serious and urgent attention to increase the facilities for training technicians.

Reorienting of a Existing Scientific Manpower

We see that average of 13 programmes are conducted each year with an average participation of 13-15 per programme. The maximum number of programmes has been in the field of Genetic engineering followed by programmes in Biochemical engineering/ enzyme engineering followed by Hybridoma tech and finally, Plant tissue culture. The field of Genetics is proving itself very efficient by the transgenic plants, vegetables, the DNA technology which is playing a major role in engineering enzymes etc. So it is quite reasonable that more number of programmes are organised in this field to help the Scientists to increase their capabilities (Table 4.6).

Table 4.6 : The Number of National and Overseas Associateships from 1986 to 2001

Sl. No.	*Year*	*National Associateships*	*Overseas Associateships*
1.	1986-87	—	15
2.	1987-88	24	17
3.	1988-89	25	20
4.	1989-90	21	25
5.	1990-91	24	27
6.	1991-92	20	25
7.	1992-93	20	20
8.	1993-94	20	25
9.	1994-95	25	23
10.	1995-96	20	26
11.	1996-97	23	25
12.	1997-98	26	26
13.	1998-99	20	25
14.	1999-00	15	20
15.	2000-01	13	22

It is observed that maximum participation is from the Universities, followed by the research institutes and finally, very meagre participation from the industries (See Table 4.7). We see that the participants from the Universities is 6 times that of industries and other private concerns, and participation of research institutes is about 4 times that of industries. The benefits of good research in the form of a good product can be only made through the industries. So the industry must be encouraged to increase their participation. This could be by involving the industries in DBT efforts, giving incentives for nominations to training, etc.

Upgrading of the Present BT Manpower

The Biotechnology associateships as seen are very important for competing at global levels. This programme plays an important role in encouraging the Scientists to upgrade their skills. The average number of National associateships has been 21 per year and average of overseas associateships has been 23 per year, over the years 1986-1999. This may indicate that provisions may be made to increase the number of associateships so that more number of scientists benefits the country by qualifying themselves to compete internationally.

Conclusion

The major points which emerge out of this present study are:

1. The present trend in the manpower coming out of the PG courses organised in various universities by DBT is following a quadratic model due to the increase in the number of institutions offering this programme over the last 10 years.
2. The Post M.Sc. & M.Tech Industrial Training is received by only a handful of students compared to the number of students who pass out every year. Even out of the students who receive training only a few get jobs.
3. Similarly it is seen that the facilities for training large number of technicians is not available. Facilities are available only to train an average 20 technicians per year.

Table 4.7 : Programmes Conducted from the year 1986-1998 in Different Areas of Biotechnology

Fields	*1986*	*1987*	*1988*	*1989*	*1990*	*1991*	*1992*	*1993*	*1994*	*1995*	*1996*	*1997*	*1998*
Genetics/Genetic Engineering	2	3	3	5	7	2	3	4	6	5	3	5	1
Hybridoma Tech/Immunodiagnostics/ Immunology	0	2	0	4	2	3	3	2	3	0	6	1	5
Plant Tissue Culture/ Plant Molecular Biology	2	2	3	2	2	4	4	4	1	3	1	1	1
Biochemical Engineering/Bioprocess Technology/Enzyme Engineering	4	4	4	3	3	6	1	4	1	3	1	2	4
Others	0	0	1	0	0	1	0	0	0				

4. The participation of industries in the short-term training programmes is very low compared to that from universities and research institutes.
5. The number of BT Associateships being provided now gives opportunities for about 20 scientists per year to work in National laboratories and about 20 to work overseas.

Suggestions to increase production of manpower with the requisite qualification:

- Universities could be informed by DBT of the possible shortages and initiate or strengthen courses which would be able to produce personnel of adequate numbers with required training.
- Mid-career training and retraining through short and mid-term training courses would be participated by the user industries who would have a say in the designing of the training courses and also co-sponsor these thereby having an opportunity to get the manpower with desired skills.
- The DBT should give very serious attention to increase facilities to train more technicians which is the need of the hour.
- Getting the Indian biotechnologists trained in BT, working abroad back through offers of attractive opportunities to invest and work.
- To facilitate efforts to increase rates of absorption of trained manpower for the jobs for which they are trained.
- Increase jobs at the level of training like initiate courses in many colleges for post-graduate diploma courses. This effort while increasing the number of personnel of required skills/ qualification available for the industries would also increase the number of jobs available for PGs in courses related to BT for the purpose of training.

5

A SURVEY OF EDUCATIONAL INFRASTRUCTURE FOR BIOTECHNOLOGY

ANALYSIS OF RESPONSES

In response to the questionnaire canvassed, the following universities in Andhra Pradesh and other States provided their feedback:

Educational Infrastructure for Biotechnology in Andhra Pradesh

Introduction

This chapter is intended to present an analysis of responses received from some institutions engaged in biotechnology education research in Andhra Pradesh and other parts of the country.

Andhra Pradesh

The responses received in the case of Andhra Pradesh could be divided into two parts: written responses and oral responses. The written responses were received from the Department of Micro Biology, University College of Science, Osmania University, Hyderabad; New Science Degree and PG College; Kakatiya University, Warangal; Biotechnology Division, Andhra University, Visakhapatnam; Indian Immunologicals Limited, Hyderabad; Shantha Biotechnics Pvt. Limited, Hyderabad and Centre for DNA Fingerprinting and Diagnostics, Hyderabad. The oral responses came through interaction with the Indian Immunological Limited, Hyderabad; Department of Biotechnology, University of Hyderabad, Hyderabad; Department of Biotechnology, Acharya N.G. Ranga Agricultural University, Hyderabad. The oral responses received in the case of Andhra Pradesh have been grouped with the oral responses received through interaction on the state of the biotechnology education existing, in general, in the country.

Table 5.1 : Universities in Andhra Pradesh who Responded to the Questionnaire

Sl. No.	*University*	*Department*
	Andhra Pradesh	
1	Osmania University, Hyderabad	Department of Microbiology Centre for Plant and Molecular Biology
2	Andhra University	Department of Biotechnology
3	SK University, Ananthapur	Department of Biotechnology
4	University of Hyderabad	Department of Life Sciences
5	Jawaharlal Nehru Technological University	Department of Biotechnology
6	NG Ranga Agricutural University	Biotech Unit
7	Sri Venkateshwara University, Tirupati	Department of Biotechnology
8	Padmavati Mahila Vishwa Vidyalaya, Tirupati	Department of Biotechnology
9	Agricultural College, Bapatla	Department of Biotechnology
10	Nagarjuna University, Guntur	Department of Biotechnology
	College	
1	New Science Degree and PG College, Warangal, AP	
	Other States	
2	Gulbarga University, Gulbarga	Department of Biotechnology
3	University of Mysore, Mysore	Department of Applied Botany
4	University of Allahabad	Centre for Biotechnology
5	Birsa Agricultural University, Ranchi	Biotechnology Centre
6	University of Mumbai, Mumbai	University Department of Chemical Technology
7	Madurai Kamraj University	Department of Plant Biotechnology
8	DSB Campus, Kumaun University	Department of Biotechnology

Affiliation Status

Out of the five organisations which furnished written responses, they were affiliated as depicted in Table 5.2 below:

Table 5.2 : Affiliation Status

No. of Institutions affiliated	*Name of the Affiliating Agency*
University College of Science, Osmania University, Hyderabad	Autonomous Educational Institute
Andhra University, Biotechnology Division	University Department
Shantha Biotechnics Pvt. Limited	Foreign Collaborator, An Indo-Oman JV Company
Indian Immunologicals Limited	A wholly owned subsidiary of National Dairy Development Board
New Science Degree and PG College, Kakatiya University, Warangal-506001	Kakatiya University, State Government
Centre for DNA Fingerprinting and Diagnostics	Department of Biotechnology, Government of India

Source: Responses received through questionnaire.

Capital Expenditure

Table 5.3 shows the amount spent on capital expenditure for infrastructure facilities (such as building, equipment, lab, computers, LAN etc.) in the year 2000-2001 and 2001-2002.

Table 5.3 : Capital Expenditure

	Name of the Organisation	*Capital Expenditure*	*2000-01*	*2001-02*
			Amount (Rs.in lakhs)	
1.	Biotechnology Division, Andhra University, Visakhapatnam	1. Equipment 2. Lab furniture 3. Chemicals 4. Glassware 5. Computers Total	Rs. 15,00,000 Rs. 5,00,000 Rs. 5,00,000 Rs. 3,00,000 Rs. 2,00,000 Rs. 30,00,000	
2.	New Science Degree and PG College, Warangal	1. Laminar Air flow 2. Culture racks and room 3. Computers Total	Rs. 50,000 Rs. 20,000 Rs. 40,000 Rs. 1,10,000	
3.	Centre for DNA Fingerprinting and Diagnostics	1. Building 2. Lab Equipment 3. Office Equipment Total	Rs. 158,00,000 Rs. 131,00,000 Rs. 158,00,000 Rs. 51,00,000 Rs. 340,00,000	Rs. 597,00,000 Rs. 95,00,000 Rs. 597,00,000 Rs. 28,00,000 Rs. 720,00,000
4.	University College of Science, Osmania University	Equipment and Books	Rs. 1,25,000	Rs. 1,25,0000
5.	Shantha Biotechnics Pvt. Ltd.	Capital Expenditure	Rs.1060,00,000	Rs. 301,00,000

Source: Responses received through questionnaire.

Academic Inputs

The various aspects of academic inputs are discussed below:

Table 5.4 shows that the Osmania, Kakatiya and Andhra Universities offer almost all the courses excepting a few. However, none of the universities are offering courses in the advanced areas such as IPRs, patenting, biodiversity, etc.

Table 5.4 : Academic Inputs

Name of the	*Osmania University*	*Kakatiya University*	*Andhra University*	*Indian Immuno-logicals Limited*	*Shantha Bio-technics Pvt. Limited*	*Centre for DNA Finger-printing and Dia-gnostics*
Genomics	√	√	—	—	—	√
Bioinformatics	√	√	—	—	—	√
Bioprospecting and Molecular Taxonomy			—	—	—	
Agriculture, Plant and Animal Biotechnology	√	√	√	—	—	√
Medicinal Biotechnology		√	√	—	—	√
Industrial Biotechnology	√	√	√	—	—	—
Bioinstrumen-tation		√	√	—	—	—
Biosafety	√	√	—	—	—	—
Ethical and Pro-prietary issues		—	—	—	—	—
Any Others		—	—	—	—	—

Source: Responses received through questionnaire.

The response relating to the issue of industry-institute interface was very varied and interesting. The institutes approach the industry to make suggestions on the formulation of syllabus. However, the industry claims that the practical training given is not upto its satisfaction. The institutes explain the reason for dissatisfaction into inadequate laboratory infrastructure and funding. The industry views the current practices adopted by institutes for summer training and project work as sub-standard. In its opinion " there is no effective mechanism for students to be sent for training in industries and research institutions during summer vacations. Barring few exceptions such as CSIR laboratories, more effective mechanisms need to be involved so that younger talent is acquainted at the right time with the requirements of industries *vis-à-vis* their career development and ambition". As per the institutes, the project work is allotted keeping in view the changing needs and requirements of the growing biotechnology industry. But the industry is of the view that the biotechnology syllabus does not incorporate knowledge of fundamentals of modern biology and chemistry. The syllabus should, therefore, aim at imparting fundamental knowledge in modern biology covering molecular biology, cell biology, microbiology, biochemistry and genetics as an integrated approach. It is also essential to ensure that the students have adequate knowledge of physics and mathematics required to study the topics covered in biotechnology. The industry appears to be more dynamic in building a rapport with the institutes. One of the respondings involved in projects such as childhood blindness, development of software and New Bone Screening with focus areas including bioinformatics and genetic diagnostics closely interact with the L.V. Prasad Eye Institute, Tata Consultancy Service and Dr. Reddy's Research Foundation for Human and Social Development. On the syllabus revision, some of the academic institutions feel that the syllabus could be revised for every 3 years.

The academic background of the faculty members/members of the staff points out that the minimum qualifications held is of the post-graduate level. The academic staff in the universities has predominance of Ph.Ds. in their faculty. The staff of the firms in the industry has a mix of both the Ph.Ds. and non-Ph.Ds. The institutions incorporated as the post-graduate colleges have also a mix of Ph.Ds. and post-graduate degrees. In the case of industry, the staff has also technicians and pharmacists. The academic institutions display the tendency of marginal additions to the academic staff while the research institutes and the firms in the industry appear to be more liberal in adding to the staff.

As far as the non-teaching staff is concerned, the departments are helped by 2-3 assistants in this category of which nominee one is the office superintendent and the other one is an attender.

Both the industry and the academic institutions appear to be shy in promoting the discipline of biotechnology by offering scholarships. Only one institution was offering six scholarships and that too sponsored by the Department of Social Welfare of the Government of Andhra Pradesh.

The institutions covered hosted a number of national and international seminars/symposiums on biotechnology related issues. The institutions offering seminar and the subjects covered by such seminars are given in Table 5.5.

Table 5.5 : International Seminars/Symposiums for the Year 2000

Sl. No.	*Name of the Organisation*	*Name of the Seminar*	*Participation Details*
1.	University College of Science, Osmania University	International Conference on Microbial Bio-technology, Trade and Public Policy	About 350 delegates from India & Abroad participated
2.	Biotechnology Division, Andhra University, Visakhapatnam	Nil	Nil
3.	Shantha Biotech Pvt. Ltd.	Nil	Nil
4.	Indian Immunologicals Limited	Nil	Nil
5.	Centre for DNA Fingerprinting and Diagnostics	• Transcription Assembly and Nucleic Acid-protein interaction • Molecular Epidemio-logy and Evolutionary Genetics of Infectious Diseases • Trends in Biochemistry • Workshop on DNA fingerprints	Organised at IISc, Bangalore Ramoji Film City, Hyderabad CDFD, Hyderabad

Source: Responses received through questionnaire.

Table 5.6 provides details of the training programmes organized to improve the quality of biotechnology research by the state level institutions. The table shows that the training

Table 5.6 : Details on Training Programmes Organized in Various Institutions for the Year 2000

Sl. No.	*Name of the Organisation*	*Name of the Seminar*	*Participation Details*
1.	University College of Science, Osmania University	Training Programmes for Collage Teachers	Duration :15 days Components: Micro-biology syllabus No.Trained:35
2.	Biotechnology Division, Andhra University, Visakhapatnam	Refresher Courses	Duration: 30 days Components: Lecturers of affiliated colleges No. Trained: 197
3.	Shantha Biotech Pvt. Ltd.	Nil	Nil
4.	Indian Immunologicals Limited	Nil	Nil
5.	Centre for DNA Fingerprinting and Diagnostics	Project Training Summer Training Winter Training	No. Trained: 29 25 11
6.	New Science Degree and PG College, Warangal	Workshop on Bio-technology for under-graduate students by Kakatiya University	Duration: 2 days Components: Tissue Culture Techniques, PCR, HPLC, DNA isolation, Gas Chromatography, Microbiology syllabus No.Trained: 25

Source: Responses received through questionnaire.

programmes organized were in the nature of refresher courses ranging from two days to one month. While the refresher courses were intended to provide a wide sweep of the problem, advance courses on topics such as microbiology, tissue culture, protoplast isolation, DNA isolation, and Gas Chromotography were organized to sensitize the participants about technical advancements. The academic institutions seek more guest lectures to satisfy the quest of biotechnology students attending the various programmes. These training programmes benefit the students in various ways. They provide sensitisation of the various issues in biotechnology, enable them to handle the equipments in the lab, and develop awareness about the current developments in biotechnology. The firms in the biotechnology industry enhance the awareness by organizing distinguished lecture series, foundation day celebrations and science day celebrations. They believe that such extension activities encourage young minds to take up careers in biotechnology and publicise their activities to people at large.

Research and Development

As a part of quality improvement among the members/students in the research institutes and institutes are subscribing various biotechnology journals and organizing better their biotech LAB with LAN, and biotech R&D unit with internet, etc.

The journals subscribed are as follows:

1. Genetic Engineering News
2. Indian Journal of Biotechnology
3. Bioinformatics
4. Vaccine
5. OIE Bulletin
6. Nature Biotechnology

Table 5.7 shows the major equipment that the institutes have in their labs for conducting research and development activities in biotechnology.

The research institutes/academic institutes responded is active in conducting collaborative research. The Indian Immunologicals Limited is conducting collaborative research and development activities with the Indian Institute of Sciences (IISc.), Bangalore, and Centre for DNA Fingerprinting and Diagnostics (CDFD), Hyderabad in the development of DNA vaccine and Molecular epidemiology, respectively. The Department of Microbiology, Osmania University, is conducting collaborative research and development activities with the Indian Institute of Chemical Technology (IICT), Hyderabad, and the International Crops Research Institute for the Semi-Arid Tropics (ICRISAT), Hyderabad in the development of studies on agriculturally important microbes.

Table 5.7 : Major Equipment

Name of the Organisation	*Equipment*
University College of Science, Osmania University	HPCL, UV-visible Spectorphotometers, lab shakers
Biotechnology Division, Andhra University,Visakhapatnam	UV-visible Spectrophotometers, High Speed refrigerators centrifuge, PCR machine, Electronic balance
Shantha Biotech Private Limited	Automatic computer controlled bioreactors Cross-flow filtration system Sophisticated computer Lyophilizer UV-VIS scanning spectrophotometer HPCL GC Liquid Scintillation Counter Thermocyclers Oligonucleotide Synthesizer Thermocyclers Tunable UV-VIS Plate Reader
Indian Immunologicals Limited	ELISA & PER Equipment Fluorescent Microscopes Spectrophotometer CO_2 Incubator, Cold store equipments, LAFUs and Centrifuges, Bioreactors
Centre for DNA Fingerprinting and Diagnostics	Automated DNA Sequence Forma CO_2 Incubator, Beckman XL-100 ultra centre fuge UV-VIS scanning spectrophotometer AB1392 DNA Synthesizer AB! Prism 7000 Real Time PCRM machine
New Science Degree and PG College, Warangal	NA

Source: Responses received through questionnaire.

Whereas academic institutions have shown no preference for building up databases for biotechnology research, the research institutes have set-up databases on structure prediction of protein and sequencing studies. The firms in the industry are of the view that the databases available at different institutions could be shared by networking the institutions.

Repositories for Biotechnology Research

On the issue as to whether the institutions responding to the questionnaire are acting as repositories for biotechnology research, the responses for mixed as shown by Table 5.8.

Table 5.8 : Repositories for Biotechnology Research

Name of the Institution Research Items	*Mono-clonal Anti-bodies*	*Nucleic Acid Probes*	*Cell Lines*	*DNA Clone Libraries*	*Germ-plasm Reposi-tories*	*Stock Centres*
Osmania University	NA	NA	NA	NA	NA	NA
Kakatiya University						
Andhra University Indian Immuno-logicals Limited	NA	NA	NA	NA	NA	NA
Shantha Bio-technics Pvt. Limited	√	√	√	√	NA	NA
Centre for DNA Fingerprinting and Diagnostics						

Source: Responses received through questionnaire.

Placement Details

The Placement constitutes the central issue in the case of professional education. Good placements attract good students and good teachers to a professional course. Both the academic institutions and industry attach a pivotal importance to placements. According to the academic institutes, the lion's share in placement goes to research labs, industry and teaching institutions. The academic institutions suggest a number of steps for strengthening the placements some of which are as follows:

1. Biotech industry should receive a serious attention for its growth and development.
2. Funding should be enhanced to strengthen the biotechnology labs.
3. Facilities for training should be developed for a better acceptability.
4. Biotech firms should provide project work to the students of undergraduate, post-graduate and research programmes.
5. Information pertaining to the qualifications and scientific (professional) background should be collected in order to provide such information to the employers.

The industry feels that the content of the training in the various programmes should be such that the requisite kind of personnel are recruited by the industry. The industry seeks the technical content in the biotechnology education.

Highlights

The following points emerge from the responses provided by the Universities in Andhra Pradesh:

- The capital expenditure for infrastructural facilities ranged from nil in few cases to around Rs. 30 lakh which included equipment cost, lab furniture, chemicals, glassware, computers etc. Over the period 2000-01 and 2001-02, the level of expenditure was more or less the same.
- Various courses offered in biotechnology and allied subjects by the universities include—Agriculture Biotechnology, Plant Biotechnology and Animal Biotechnology, Industrial and Engineering Biotechnology, Downstream Processing in Biotechnology, Biochemistry and Microbiology, Transport Phenomena and Separation

Processes, Adsorptive and Chromatographic Separations, Laboratory Techniques in Biotechnology, Genomics, Bioinformatics, Medicinal Biotechnology, Biosafety, Ethical and Proprietary Issues, Microbial Technology and Biodiversity.

- In most of the cases, the syllabus is revised once in three years and annually in few cases. Although students have been consulted in most cases on the revision of syllabus, there is not much progress in this direction. Similarly, interaction with the industry is at a meagre level. Although there are tie-ups with the Industry, there is no active collaboration going on and at the most the students are provided with a few projects which are very preliminary in nature and does not lead to any serious application.
- The strength of the faculty ranges from three to seven per department and over the one-year period 1999-2000 to 2000-2001, the figures are more or less the same. In most of the cases, there is a formidable presence of supporting staff.
- Most of the respondent Universities have faculty visiting them from various related departments such as botany, zoology, environmental sciences, pharmaceutical sciences and statistics. Experts are also drawn from the industry and foreign universities.
- Refresher courses are being offered by some universities for lecturers of affiliated colleges. Other extension programmes are being conducted through consultancy and guest lectures outside. Most of the respondents feel that such training programmes help in updating the existing knowledge on the subject, increase the intensity and level of interaction with the industry and provide inspiration for carrying out research projects. It also provides an opportunity to scientists, policy makers, and beneficiaries to come to a common platform and exchange their views.
- It has been felt that bioinformatics, genomics and proteomics need to be added to the existing curriculum.

- In nearly 50 per cent of the cases, there are no scholarships for pursuing biotechnology and related disciplines in the universities. There are studentships given in few cases sponsored by the DBT, Government of India. In one case, the university has provided one scholarship each for rank holder at post-graduate/M.Sc., M.Phil and Ph.D. level.
- Universities have followed the tradition of organizing national and international seminars and symposia on biotechnology wherein experts from other countries also participate. This has been a common trend across all the universities.
- Active interaction with Industry and R&D support is present in one or two cases and lacking completely in most of the cases.
- The lab facilities currently existing in the universities include, tissue culture lab to conduct protocol development for propagation, microbiology for industrial microbiology research, fermentation lab for enzyme production, large scale fermentation, food biotechnology lab for enzyme modifications, applications etc., pharmaceutical biotechnology for synthesis of chiral compounds using enzymes, microbes, plant tissue culture for synthesis of flavour, perfumery compounds using plant tissue culture, affinity chromatography and separation labs for separation and purification of metabolites, enzymes and developing new ligands for chromatography, supercritical and other extractions lab for extraction, purification of metabolites by supercritical, ultrasonic and other recent techniques, biotech lab for industrial biotech research and downstream processing.
- Some of the major scientific equipments listed out by the respondents include HPLC, HPTLC, GC, UV Spectrometer, Electrophoretic Apparatus, Super Centrifuge, Environment Chamber, Ultra Low Deep Freezer, Gaulin Homogenizer, Bioreactor and Photo bioreactors, Sonifier, Liquid Chromatography Unit, Lab

Scale and Pilot Scale Fermentors (15 to 65 litres, Chemap, Electrolab etc.), Electron Microscope, Bio profile system etc.

- Only a few universities have separate computer hardware and software facilities for their biotechnology centre. Among them only a couple of universities have provided access to internet and LAN in their biotech units.
- Most of the universities are subscribing biotech related journals and magazines. However, online and off-line computer databases are non-existent but for a few universities.
- As per the responses, under the repositories for biotechnology research, the following shared resources for biotechnology research are available at few universities: nucleic acid probes, DNA clone libraries and microbial stock cultures.
- Only one university has reported the status of placements of students in biotechnology. The number of placements at the post-graduate level average out to 6 in the research labs, 3 in the industry, 4 in affiliated colleges. The placement scenario has been similar for 1991-2000 and 2000-2001 in this case.

Analysis of Responses from Research Institutions and Firms

The following research institutes and firms responded to the questionnaire:

Table 5.9 : Research Institutions which Responded to the Questionnaire

Sl. No.	*Research Institution*
1.	Centre for Cellular and Molecular Biology, Hyderabad
2.	Indian Institute of Chemical Technology, Hyderabad
3.	National Institute of Nutrition, Hyderabad
4.	Indian Immunologicals Limited, Hyderabad

Table 5.10 : Research Firms which Responded to the Questionnaire

Sl. No.	*Industrial R&D Units*
1.	Dr. Reddy's Laboratories, Hyderabad
2.	i-Labs, Hyderabad
3.	LV Prasad Eye Institute, Hyderabad
4.	Shantha Biotech, Hyderabad
5.	Biological E Limited, Hyderabad
6.	ICICI Knowledge Park, Hyderabad
7.	Shapoorji Pallonji Biotech Park Limited, Hyderabad
8.	Ernst & Young, Hyderabad

The following points emerge from the responses provided by the research institutions and industrial R&D units dealing with biotechnology:

- Across all the research institutions and industrial R&D units, an increasing trend in the scientific and technical personnel involved in biotechnology research has been observed.
- However, the level of industry-academia interaction and industry support to students is very low. As far as training programmes are concerned, there is no effective mechanism for students to be sent for training in industries and research institutions. Barring few exceptions such as CSIR Labs, more effective mechanisms need to be evolved so that younger talent is acquainted at the right time with the requirements of industries *vis-à-vis* their career development and ambition.
- In order to plan biotechnology well, the industrial R&D units have the perception that the syllabus should aim at imparting fundamental knowledge in modern biology covering molecular biology, cell biology, microbiology, biochemistry, and genetics as an integrated approach. It is also essential that the students have adequate knowledge of physics and mathematics required to study the topics covered in biotechnology.

- The major scientific equipments available at the R&D units include automatic computer controlled bio-reactors of various capacities from 10 L to 100 L for microbial and mammalian cell culture, provided with state-of-the-art accessories for exhaust gas analysis, perfusion and online nutrient and metabolite analysis. Cross-flow filtration systems of various types such as membrane, hollow fibre and ceramic for handling filtration processes upto a volume of 1000 L, continuous centrifuge for handling large-scale separation processes upto a volume of 500 L, homogenisers including a bead-mill and a high-pressure homogenizer for pilot scale cell disruption, sophisticated computer controlled chromatography systems for laboratory and pilot scale protein purification along with axial and radial flow and expanded bed columns of various sizes, pilot scale lyophilizer for aseptic freeze-drying, dry heat and steam sterilizing equipment, florescence and phase-contrast microscopes with camera and video attachments, scanning densitometer, gel documentation system, UV-VIS spectrophotometer, Spectroflouimeter, HPCL, GC, Liquid Scintillation Counter, Oligonucleotide Synthesizer, Thermocyclers, Tunable UV-VIS Plate Reader, Automated DNA Sequencer, SD200 Spectral Karyotype System, Beekman XL-100 Ultra Centre, UV-VIS Scanning Spectrophotometer, AB1392 DNA synthesizer, ABI Prism 7000 Real Time PCR Machine, ELISA & PBR Equipment, Fluorescent Microscopes, Spectrophotometer and CO_2 incubators.
- In most of the cases, Internet facility is accessible to all the research centres. Scientific and technical data availability has been indicated for areas such as federal and state regulations on Biosafety and reference standards for quality assurance of biotechnology based measurements.

Responses from Institutions from States other than Andhra Pradesh

The institutions responding to the questionnaire from the States other than Andhra Pradesh include the Department of Applied Botany and Biotechnology, University of Mysore, Karnataka; Centre for Biotechnology, University of Allahabad, Uttar Pradesh; Biotechnology Centre, Birsa Agricultural University, Ranchi (Jharkhand); Department of Biotechnology, Kumaun University, Nainital, Uttaranchal; Department of Chemical Technology, University of Mumbai, Mumbai, Maharashtra; and Department of Biotechnology, Gulbarga University, Gulbarga, Karnataka.

Affiliation Status

The affiliation status of the responding institutions was as follows:

Table 5.11 : Affiliation Status

Sl. No.	*Name of the Institution*	*Name of the Affiliating Agency*
1.	Mysore University	Government of Karnataka
2.	Gulbarga University	Affiliated to Government of Karnataka, DBT, GoI, and UGC
3.	Allahabad University	Affiliated to State Government, and AICTE
4.	Birsa University	State Government and Government of India
5.	Kumaun University	
6.	Mumbai University	Affiliated to UGC

Source: Responses received through questionnaire.

It is clear from Table 5.11 that all the six departments covered were affiliated to their respective universities and thereby the State Governments. However, the Department of Biotechnology, Gulbarga Universitity had affiliation to the Government of India and the UGC also. The Birsa Agricultural University, Ranchi (Jharkhand) was affiliated to the Central Government.

Capital Expenditure

The items of capital expenditure incurred by the departments under reference including building, equipment, lab, computers, LAN etc. in the year 2000-2001 and 2001-2002. Table 5.12 shows the amount spent on these items:

Table 5.12 : Capital Expenditure

Sl. No.	*Name of the Institution*	*Capital Expenditure*	*2000-01* Amount (Rs.in lakhs)	*2001-02*
1.	Mysore University	Building Equipment Lab LAN Total	Rs. 3.00 Rs. 30.00 Rs. 3.00 Rs. 3.00 Rs. 39.00	
2.	Gulbarga University	Scientific Equipment Computer, LAN Remodelling of Lab Total	Rs. 4.00 Rs. 3.00 Rs. 1.00 Rs. 8.00	
3.	Allahabad University	NA		
4.	Birsa University	Total	Rs.11,10,755	Rs. 1,93,809
5.	Kumaun University			
6.	Mumbai University	No Expenditure		

Source: Responses received through questionnaire.

The table shows that whereas some departments incurred expenditure on capital items, there were other which did not spent any money at all. This happened due to the setting up of the department much earlier which obviated the need to incur capital expenditure on any item included under the study.

Academic Inputs

The various aspects of academic inputs are discussed below:

Table 5.13 : Academic Inputs

Name of the Institutions → *Courses ↓*	*Mysore University*	*Gulbarga University*	*Allahabad University*	*Ranchi University*	*Kumaun University*	*Mumbai University*
Genomics	√	√	√			√
Bioinformatics	√	√	√			
Bioprospecting and Molecular Taxonomy						
Agriculture, Plant and Animal Biotechnology	√	√	√	√		√
Medicinal Biotechnology		√	√			√
Industrial biotechnology	√	√	√			√
Bio-instrumentation			√			
Biosafety		√	√		√	√
Ethical and Proprietary issues	√	√	√			√
Any Others		√ Microbial Tech, Immunotechnology and Biodiversity				√ IPRs Patents, Environmental Safety

Source: Responses received through questionnaire.

Table 5.13 shows that the universities starting the biotechnology courses during the recent years, were offering only one or two specializations. The table also shows that some universities are trying to incorporate new courses such as IPRs, Patents, Environmental Safety, Immunotechnology and Biodiversity.

The biotechnology departments covered under the study

of certain essential facilities. Ultimately it is observed that students are obliged to make do with facilities that fall short of their need and expectations. Further, no planned efforts are undertaken to nurture, develop and upgrade biotechnology department in terms of proficiency of teachers, lab facilities, and library and industry interaction.

Students

Students of biotechnology courses are unlike those in the other M.Sc. courses in that they do not usually possess the vertical UG background. For instance, most students in M.Sc. (Microbiology) would possess an undergraduate degree in microbiology.

Teacher

There are a number of dimensions of teacher related problems.

Qualification and Workload

Teachers teaching in most of the biotechnology courses are not those who have been appointed on a permanent basis but rather gathered from various departments. The problem is further compounded by the question as to how well qualified are most of these teachers to teach in biotechnology courses.

Secondly, the workload, though in terms of norms is supposed to be 16 hours per week per faculty member, actually exceeds the norm by nearly 50 to 100 per cent mainly due to the requirements of lab work, lack of support from qualified technical staff and more number of students per batch than should be logically allocated.

A post-graduate biotechnology class should have ideally a minimum of 10 to a maximum of 15 students. But this is very rarely the case. The need to make sure that the courses are run self-financed or secure a surplus, forces many academic institutions forces institutions offering courses in biotechnology to admit a very large number of students. This reduces one to one interaction required between the teachers and taught which is so essential for this course.

Workshops and Refresher Courses

The demand of biotechnologists as such in India has increased only, of late, in spite of the fact that research in this field has made in-roads for quite some time. Senior teachers, specifically in this field, who would act as mentors to the newly admitted students are not very easy to come by making the task of the teaching staff cumbersome and difficult. The DBT and UGC have not mounted vigorously refresher courses for the teachers, which could help them orient and update them to the expectations. Infact, the biotechnology is one field that would require frequent refresher programmes owing to continuous advancement in research in this field.

Remuneration

The lecturership packages offered in general in the science stream is by no means fair. At the outset, the courses like bio chemistry, microbiology and biotechnology in most colleges are not government funded like those of botany, zoology, chemistry and physics so most of the teaching staffs are not permanent employees but are rather appointed on a temporary basis (more appropriately as contract employees). The contracts are usually drawn for the academic year and terminated when the colleges close for the summer vacation. The employees have to seek their own means of remuneration during this period. The renewal of the contract is decided entirely by the management and no explanations are offered whatsoever if a particular staff is not inducted back again. This shabby treatment meted out to members offers very little encouragement to young aspirants who wish to take up a teaching job in biotechnology.

Syllabus

The lack or continuity between the undergraduate and post-graduate course requires that a basic orientation course be instituted to familiarize the students to the curriculum, which is not offered by the universities.

There is a lot of disparity in the post-graduate course syllabus in biotechnology of the various universities. Some universities offer courses in the nature of a master's degree without doing full justice by linking it to an undergraduate programme. The syllabus are inadequate in terms of contents and their topicality. The curriculum for the B.Sc. course in biotechnology was provided by the UGC, adopted by the BU with certain changes, nearly a decade ago. This is inadequate in the context of the present state of knowledge of the subject. It is also divorced from ground realities, as it does not leave scope to educate on the issues that are currently hotly debated.

Although the syllabus includes a paper on bioinformatics in most of the universities, not much is done due to the absence of hardware and software and also the requisite equipments. No space is created in syllabus for vocational education in biotechnology. The kind of graduates turned out by the educational institutions are not acceptable to the industry because they are largely 'unemployable'. There is need for a comprehensive over view of biotechnology education in the country and an over skill will only spoil the party.

Conclusion

Although biotechnology holds key to a brighter future of India, the biotechnology education does not reinforce this assertion. The biotechnology education suffers from a number of serious shortcomings as related to the content, spread, pedagogy, intake, admission systems and procedures, topicality, industry demands and the purveyor. The infrastructure facilities in terms of equipments, lab layout and the technicians continue to remain substandard. Though India has established a global outreach in biotechnology, it needs to consolidate the position both at home and abroad.

7

SUGGESTIONS AND RECOMMENDATIONS

General Recommendations

- Evolving a specific policy on biotechnology education.
- Facilitating growth of a supportive, thriving intellectual climate for development of biotechnology education.
- Encourage research and higher education in biotechnology to provide well trained professionals in biotechnology education.
- Initiate programmes to provide retraining and inter-disciplinary training to scientists and technical and vocational staff.
- Provide adequate funding for improving facilities in universities and colleges across all the departments.
- Check the deterioration in existing facilities and lack of funds for new facilities for biotechnology research limits the progress.
- Coordinate efforts to upgrade research facilities in universities and educational institutions.
- Maintain operate high grade equipment and instrumentation to support research of high caliber which are expensive and difficult to acquire.
- Provide funding for state-of-the-art equipment for biotechnology research and make it available to the academic institutions.
- Arrange resource sharing facility for the institutions with research labs and industry groups.
- Organise programmes needed to enhance public literacy

concerning biotechnology, as well as to attract and retain students in biotechnology related science and engineering through pre and post-doctoral levels and retain individuals with experience in other disciplines for career in biotechnology.

Admissions

- The number of students admitted in the biotechnology courses at all the levels far exceeds the sanctioned strength of the institution.
- Uniform norms to be laid out by the educational institutions with regard to the selection of candidates for various graduate and post-graduate courses in biotechnology.
- The management of these institutions would ultimately be the deciding factor on the candidatures thus giving way to a dilution in the quality of the students at these courses.

Fee Structure

- The huge fee structures of the various biotechnology courses which vary from Rs. 5,000 to Rs. 10,000 at the university offered courses and from Rs. 50,000 per annum to Rs. 1.2 lakh per annum in private colleges affiliated to the various universities deprive a financially weak student to join the course.

Infrastructure

- Mushrooming of biotechnology colleges to be stopped immediately.
- The infrastructure available in the educational institutions to provide instructions in biotechnology is not adequate to cater to the intake admitted.
- Excessive intake of students results in a decline in quality of the end product. Primarily, the infrastructure rarely allows the students to have hands on experience.

- These shortcomings lead to a turnout of biotechnology graduates and post-graduates ill-equipped both in theory and practice.
- The academic audit wings in the universities should ensure the availability of the requisite lab space, instrumentation facilities and qualification of the teaching staff.
- There occurs at some stage a compromise to high standards, eventually resulting in deficiency of certain essential facilities.
- Ultimately it is observed that students are obliged to make do with facilities that fall short of their need and expectations.
- Further, no planned efforts are undertaken to nurture, develop and upgrade biotechnology department in terms of proficiency of teachers, lab facilities, and library and industry interaction.
- The lab facilities currently existing in the universities include, tissue culture lab to conduct protocol development for propagation, microbiology for industrial microbiology research, fermentation lab for enzyme production, large scale fermentation, food biotechnology lab for enzyme modifications, applications etc., pharmaceutical biotechnology for synthesis of chiral compounds using enzymes, microbes, plant tissue culture for synthesis of flavour, perfumery compounds using plant tissue culture, affinity chromatography and separations lab for separation and purification of metabolites, enzymes and developing new ligands for chromatography, supercritical and other extractions lab for extraction, purification of metabolites by supercritical, ultrasonic and other recent techniques, biotech lab for industrial biotech research and downstream processing.
- Some of the major scientific equipments listed out by the respondents include HPLC, HPTLC, GC, UV Spectrometer, Electrophoretic Apparatus, Super Centrifuge, Environment Chamber, Ultra Low Deep Freezer, Gaulin Homogenizer, Bioreactor and Photo bioreactors, Sonifier, Liquid Chromatography Unit, Lab Scale and Pilot Scale Fermentors (15 to 65 litres, Chemap, Electrolab etc.), Electron Microscope, Bio-profile System etc.
- Only a few universities have separate computer hardware and software facilities for their biotechnology centre. Among

them only a couple of universities have provided access to internet and LAN in their biotech units.

- Most of the universities are subscribing biotech related journals and magazines. However, online and off-line computer databases are non-existent but for a few universities.
- As per the responses, under the repositories for biotechnology research, the following shared resources for biotechnology research are available at few universities: nucleic acid probes, DNA clone libraries and microbial stock cultures.

Scholarships and Assistants

- In nearly 50 per cent of the cases, there are no scholarships for pursuing biotechnology and related disciplines in the universities. There are studentships given in few cases sponsored by the DBT, Government of India. In one case, the university has provided one scholarship each for rank holder at post-graduate/M.Sc., M.Phil and Ph.D. level.
- Universities have followed the tradition of organizing national and international seminars and symposia on biotechnology wherein experts from other countries also participate. This has been a common trend across all the universities.
- Active interaction with Industry and R&D support is present in one or two cases and lacking completely in most of the cases.
- However, the level of industry-academia interaction and industry support to students is very low. As far as training programmes are concerned, there is no effective mechanism for students to be sent for training in industries and research institutions. Barring few exceptions such as CSIR Labs, more effective mechanisms need to be evolved so that younger talent is acquainted at the right time with the requirements of industries *vis-à-vis* their career development and ambition.

Placements

- Only one university has reported the status of placements of students in biotechnology. The number of placements at the post-graduate level average out to 6 in the research labs, 3 in the industry, 4 in affiliated colleges. The placement scenario has been similar for 1991-2000 and 2000-2001 in this case.

Biotechnology Education and Faculty

- The strength of the faculty ranges from three to seven per department and over the one-year period 1999-2000 to 2000-2001, the figures are more or less the same. In most of the cases, there is a formidable presence of supporting staff.
- Most of the respondent universities have faculty visiting them from various related departments such as botany, zoology, environmental sciences, pharmaceutical sciences and statistics. Experts are also drawn from the industry and foreign universities.
- Refresher courses are being offered by some universities for lecturers of affiliated colleges. Other extension programmes are being conducted through consultancy and guest lectures outside. Most of the respondents feel that such training programmes help in updating the existing knowledge on the subject, increase the intensity and level of interaction with the industry and provide inspiration for carrying out research projects. It also provides an opportunity to scientists, policy makers, and beneficiaries to come to a common platform and exchange their views.

Qualification and Workload

- Teachers teaching in most of the biotechnology courses are not those who have been appointed on a permanent basis but rather gathered from various departments.
- The problem is further compounded by the question as to how well qualified are most of these teachers to teach in biotechnology courses.
- Secondly the workload, though in terms of norms is supposed to be 16 hours per week per faculty member, actually exceeds

the norm by nearly 50 to 100 per cent mainly due to the requirements of lab work, lack of support from qualified technical staff and more number of students per batch than should be logically allocated.

- A post-graduate biotechnology class should have ideally a minimum of 10 to a maximum of 15 students. But this is very rarely the case. The need to make sure that the courses are run self-financed or secure a surplus, forces many academic institutions forces institutions offering courses in biotechnology to admit a very large number of students.
- This reduces one to one interaction required between the teachers and taught which is so essential for this course.

Workshops and Refresher Courses

- The demand of biotechnologists as such in India has increased only, of late, in spite of the fact that research in this field has made in-roads for quite some time.
- Senior teachers, specifically in this field, who would act as mentors to the newly admitted students are not very easy to come by making the task of the teaching staff cumbersome and difficult.
- The DBT and UGC have not mounted vigorously refresher courses for the teachers, which could help them orient and update them to the expectations.
- Infact, the biotechnology is one field that would require frequent refresher programmes owing to continuous advancement in research in this field.

Remuneration

- The lecturership packages offered in general in the science stream is by no means fair.
- At the outset, the courses like bio-chemistry, microbiology and biotechnology in most colleges are not government funded like those of botany, zoology, chemistry and physics so most of the teaching staffs are not permanent employees

but are rather appointed on a temporary basis, (more appropriately as contract employees).

- The contracts are usually drawn for the academic year and terminated when the colleges close for the summer vacation.
- The employees have to seek their own means of remuneration during this period. The renewal of the contract is decided entirely by the management and no explanations are offered whatsoever if a particular staff is not inducted back again.
- This shabby treatment meted out to members offers very little encouragement to young aspirants who wish to take up a teaching job in biotechnology.

Syllabus

- A comprehensive syllabus is a prerequisite for bringing in greater credibility for the course.
- The syllabus to be in tune with the latest development in biotech field to make the students employable and acceptable to the market.
- Need to create greater space for vocational education in biotechnology.
- A basic orientation course to be instituted to bring in continuity between the undergraduate and post-graduate course to familiarize the students to the curriculum, which is not offered by the universities.
- Various courses offered in biotechnology and allied subjects by the universities include—Agriculture Biotechnology, Plan Biotechnology and Animal Biotechnology, Industrial and Engineering Biotechnology, Downstream Processing in Biotechnology, Biochemistry and Microbiology, Transport Phenomena and Separation Processes, Adsorptive and Chromatographic Separations, Laboratory Techniques in Biotechnology, Genomics, Bioinformatics, Medicinal Biotechnology, Biosafety, Ethical and Proprietary Issues, Microbial Technology and Biodiversity.
- In most of the cases, the syllabus is revised once in three years and annually in few cases. Although students have

been consulted in most cases on the revision of syllabus, there is not much progress in this direction. Similarly, interaction with the industry is at a meagre level. Although there are tie-ups with the Industry, there is no active collaboration going on and at the most the students are provided with a few projects which are very preliminary in nature and does not lead to any serious application.

- It has been felt that bioinformatics, genomics and proteomics need to be added to the existing curriculum.
- In order to plan biotechnology well, the industrial R&D units have the perception that the syllabus should aim at imparting fundamental knowledge in modern biology covering molecular biology, cell biology, microbiology, biochemistry, and genetics as an integrated approach. It is also essential that the students have adequate knowledge of physics and mathematics required to study the topics covered in biotechnology.
- Some of the cutting-edge modules that could be included in biotechnology education and training programmes are: Basic Biology (Microbiology, Cell Biology, Biochemistry, etc.); Introduction to Computation/Information Theory; Genomics; Proteomics; Introduction to Algorithms; Introduction to Artificial Intelligence; Introduction to Microarrays; Computational Molecular Biology; Fourier Transformation, Hidden Markov Models, Fuzzy Logic, Biopackages—BioPerl, BioJava; Molecular Modelling and Drug Design; Neuroinformatics; and Cheminformatics.

ANNEXURES

ANNEXURE I

EDUCATIONAL INFRASTRUCTURE FOR BIOTECHNOLOGY

Section 1: General Information

1. Name of the Organisation: ....

2. Address: ....

3. Year of establishment: ....

4. The Organisation is affiliated to/associated with/comes under the:

Sl. No.		*Please* (√)	*Please Give Details*
1	State Government		
2	Government of India		
3	CSIR		
4	UGC		
5	AICTE		
6	Foreign Collaborator(s)		
7	Corporate House(s)		
8	Others		

5. Please indicate the amount spent on capital expenditure for infrastructure facilities (such as, building, equipment, lab, computers, LAN etc.) in the year 2000-2001 and 2001-2002:

Sl. No	*Item*	*Expenditure (in Rs.)*
1		
2		
3		
4		
5		
6		

Section 2: Academic Inputs

1. Please provide details of the Courses in Biotechnology being offered by your Organisation covering the following fields:

   (a) Genomics
   (b) Bioinformatics
   (c) Bioprospecting and Molecular Taxonomy
   (d) Agriculture, Plant and Animal Biotechnology
   (e) Medicinal Biotechnology
   (f) Industrial Biotechnology
   (g) Bioinstrumentation
   (h) Biosafety
   (i) Ethical and Proprietary issues
   (k) Any other

2. Please provide details of revision of syllabus on biotechnology? What is the process for revision and benchmarking?
3. Please provide details of feedback from students on updating the course?
4. Please provide details on the industry-institution interface on updating syllabus?
5. Please provide details of faculty in biotechnology.

Year	*Name of the Faculty*	*Educational Background*	*Designation*
1999-2000			
1.			
2.			
3.			
4.			
5.			
6.			
7.			
2000-2001			
1.			
2.			
3.			
4.			
5.			
6.			
7.			

6. Please provide details of the faculty exchange programmes, expert guest lectures etc. for biotechnology teaching staff.
7. Please provide details of the non-teaching/Administrative staff in biotechnology.

Sl. No.	*Name*	*Background*	*Designation*

8. Please provide details of scholarships constituted at the institute for promoting biotechnology study in India and abroad.

Year	*Number of scholarships offered*	*Nature of scholarship*	*Duration*
1999-2000			
1.			
2.			
3.			
2000-2001			
1.			
2.			
3.			

9. Please provide details of the National and International Seminars/Symposia organised by your institution on biotechnology related issues.

Year	*Name of the Seminar/Symposia*	*Participation details*

10. Please provide details of the training programmes organised to improve the quality of biotechnology research.

Sl. No	*Name Programme*	*Duration*	*Components*	*Number Trained*

11. Please give details of the industry support to the institution in promoting biotechnology education.

Sl. No	*Name of the industry*	*Nature of support*

12. Please provide details of extension/awareness programmes on biotechnology initiated by your institution.

1.
2.
3.
4.
5.
6.

13. Please list down the advantages by organising training programmes, seminars, symposia etc.

1.
2.
3.
4.

14. Please give suggestions on updating the syllabus on biotechnology.

Section 3: Information on Research and Development in Biotechnology

1. Month and year of set up of Biotech Research & Development (R&D) Unit
2. Location of the Unit
3. Expenditure on Biotech R&D (in lakhs)

Year	*1996-97*	*1997-1998*	*1998-1999*	*1999-2000*	*2000-2001*

4. Please specify the number of labs in the biotech R&D unit?

Sl. No.	*Name of the Lab*	*Type of Research Undertaken*	*No. of Personnel Attached*

5. What is the average number of personal computers available per lab?
   (a) Does the biotech Lab have a LAN?
   (b) Does the biotech R&D unit have access to Internet?
6. What is the number of referred journals on Biotechnology available in the library? Please specify?
   (a)
   (b)
   (c)
   (d)

7. Does your library have a networking with other Biotechnology R&D centres/Biotech Parks elsewhere in the country?

Sl. No	Name of the centre	Nature of Collaboration

8. What are the major scientific equipment's available at your R&D unit? Please specify.

Major Equipment	Name of the Lab

9. Please provide details of any R&D collaboration with In-house R&D units of the public and private biotech enterprises?

Sl. No	Collaborating Unit	Nature of Collaboration

10. Please provide details of research arrangements with other labs in utilisation/sharing of scientific infrastructure.

11. Please give your suggestions on R&D facilities necessary for biotechnology.

Section 4: Database for Biotechnology Research

1. Please provide details regarding the acquisition of databases and information sources for biotechnology research at the institution? (Journals, Magazines etc.)
2. Please provide details regarding access of databases and information sources for biotechnology research at the institution? (Computerised cataloguing, online information etc.)
3. Please provide details regarding the expansion maintenance and cataloging of databases/information sources? (Expenditure in the Plan Grant etc.)
4. Please provide the details on the scientific/technical data available on the following areas:

Sl. No	*Area-wise Details*	*Available/Not Available*
1.	Genetics	
2.	Proteins	
3.	DNS sequences and profiles	
4.	Bioenergetics	
5.	Germplasm	
6.	Genomic maps	
7.	Federal and state regulations on biosafety	
8.	Reference standards for quality assurance of biotechnology based measurements	

5. Please provide suggestions on how to improve the database for biotechnology research.

Section 5: Repositories for Biotechnology Research

1. Please provide details regarding the shared resources for biotechnology research available at the institution.

(a) Does your institution have banks of monoclonal antibodies?
(b) Does your institution have nucleic acid probes?
(c) Does your institution have cell lines?
(d) Does your institution have DNA clone libraries?
(e) Does your institution have Germplasm Repositories?
(f) Does your institution have stock centres?

Section 6 : Placement Details

1. Please provide the details of placements at the postgraduate/ research levels in the field of biotechnology.

Year	*Number of placements*	*Company details*	*Duration*
1999-2000			
1.			
2.			
3.			
2000-2001			
1.			
2.			
3.			

2. Please give suggestions to improve the placement prospects in biotechnology.

Mailing address:

Prof. R. K. Mishra
Dean (Research)
Institute of Public Enterprise
Osmania University Campus
Hyderabad- 500 007
Tel: 7098145, 7097445
Fax: 7095478
Email: rkmishra_99_1999@yahoo.com

ANNEXURE II

LIST OF COORDINATORS—DBT SPONSORED UNIVERSITIES/INSTITUTIONS OFFERING REGULAR TEACHING & TRAINING COURSES IN BIOTECHNOLOGY IN INDIA

M.Sc. General Biotechnology (2-year courses)

Dr. Uttam Pati,
Chairman,
Centre for Biotechnology,
Jawaharlal Nehru University,
New Mehrauli Road,
New Delhi-110 067
Tel: 6167261 (O) direct
6183633 (O)
Fax: 6198234
Email: uttam@jnuriv.ernet.in

Prof. K. Veluthambi
Head & Coordinator,
School for Biotechnology,
Madurai Kamraj University,
Madurai-625 021
Tel: 0452-858683, 858415
Fax: 0452-859105
Email: veluthambi@mrna.tn.nic.in

Prof. B.B. Chattoo,
Coordinator,
Biotechnology Centre,
Dept. of Microbiology,
Faculty of Science,
MS. University of Baroda,
Baroda-390 002
Tel: 0265-794396 (O)
794919 (R)
Fax: 0265-792508
Email: shahak@hotmail.com

Prof. V. Sitaramam
Biotechnology Department,
University of Pune,
Ganeshkhind,
Pune-411 007
Tel: 020-5655179, 5654952 (dir),
5655185 (R),
Mobile-9822017758
Fax: 020-5651821, 5655179
Email: sitaram@unipune.ernet.in

Prof. B.D. Singh
School of Biotechnology,
Faculty of Sciences,
Banaras Hindu University,
Varanasi-221 005
Tel: 0542-317331, 307314, 307315,
316641 (R)
Fax: 0542-316693, 317074
Email: brahmadsingh@hotmail.com

Prof. S. Durani
Convener,
Biotechnology Centre,
Indian Institute of Technology, Powai,
Mumbai-400 076
Tel: 022-5767164, 5767770 (dir.)-
Ext. 3729 (O), 3134 (L),5768164 (R)
Fax: 022-5783480
Email: sdurani@btc.iitb.ernet.in

Dr. Ben M.J. Pereira
Prof. & Head,
Department of Bioscience &
Biotechnology,
Roorkee University,
Roorkee—247667
Tel: 01332-85216 (O), 72804 (R),
85118 (R), 85790 (lab)
Fax: 01332-73560
Email: pereira@rurkiu.ernet.in

Prof. M. Saleemuddin
Coordinator Inter-disciplinary,
Biotechnology Unit,
Aligarh Muslim University,
Aligarh-202 002
Tel: 0571-401718 (O), 401979 (O)
Fax: 0571-401081
Email: btisamu@x400.nicgw.nic.in

Dr. S.S. Bhullar
Reader & Head,
Department of Biotechnology,
Guru Nanak Dev University,
Amritsar-143 005
Tel: 0183-258802-09, 3177 (O),
256011 (R)
Fax: 0183-258272, 258820
Email: ssbhullar@goplay.com,
Bhullarss@yahoo.com

Prof. Anil Kumar
Head School of Biotechnology,
Vigyan Bhavan,
Devi Ahilya Vishwavidyalaya,
Khandwa Road,
Indore-452 001
Tel: 0731-470372 (O), 470373 (O)
Fax: 0731-470372
Email: bioinfo@bom4.vsnl.net.in

Prof. K. Subba Rao
Coordinator,
Biotechnology Programme,
School of Life Sciences,
University of Hyderabad,
Hyderabad-500 134
Tel: 040-3010451 (O), 3010256 (R)
Fax: 040-3010120, 145, 451
Email: ksrsl@uohyd.ernet.in

Prof. T.C. Bhalla
Chairman, Dept. of Biotechnology,
Himachal Pradesh University,
Summer Hill,
Shimla-171 005
Himachal Pradesh
Tel: 0177-231948 (O), 230573(R)
Fax: 0177-230775
Email:hp.university@x400.nicgw.nic.in

Dr. M.V. Joseph
Reader & Head,
Dept. of Biotechnology,
University of Calicut,
Calicut University P.O.,
Kerala-673 635
Tel: 0494-401144-Ext.403, 404,
401159 (dir), 401500(R)
Fax: 0494-400269
Email: biotech@unical.ac.in

Dr.Vinay Sharma
Head, Dept. of Biosciences and
Biotechnology,
Banasthali Vidyapeeth,
P.O.Banasthali Vidyapeeth,
Banasthali-340 022
(Rajasthan)
Tel: 01438-28456 (O), 28341 ext. 280,
28533(R)
Fax: 01438-28365
Email: vinaysharma@hotmail.com

Dr. A.K. Buragohain
Department of Molecular Biology and
Biotechnology,
Tezpur University P.B.72,
P.O.Tezpur Distt. Sonitpur,
Assam-784 001

Prof. G.R. Naik
Chairman,
Dept. of Biotechnology,
Gulbarga University,
Gulbarga-585 106
Tel: 08472-45781 (O), 45337 (R)
Fax: 08472-45632
Email: grnaik@hotmail.com

Dr. A.K. Koul
Director
Dept. of Biotechnology,
University of Jammu,
Ambedkar Road,
Jammu Tawi-180 004
Tel: 0191-535248/302 (extn.)
554976 (R)
Fax: 0191-548607
Fax: Registrar-431365 (O)
Fax: Controller-432856 (O),
431627 (R)

Dr. Manoj Dhar
Head, DBT,
University of Jammu,
Ambedkar Road,
Jammu Tawi-180 004
Tel: 0191-456534 (O)
Fax: 0191-548607
Fax: Registrar-431365 (O)
Fax: Controller-432856 (O),
431627 (R)

Prof. Y.K. Aggrawal
Coordinator,
School of Science,
Gujarat University,
Ahmedabad-380 009
Tel: 079-6300969 (O), 6308545 (O),
6302200 (R)
Fax: 079-6308545

Prof. H.S. Prakash
Professor,
Dept. of Applied Botany and
Biotechnology,
University of Mysore,
Manasgangotri,
Mysore-570 006
Tel: 0821-515126 (O), 517577 (R)
Fax: 0821-411467
Email: seedpath@bgl.vsnl.net.in

Prof. (Mrs.) Krishna Misra
Coordinator, Centre for Biotechnology,
Dept. of Chemistry,
University of Allahabad,
Allahabad-211 002
Tel: 0532-465462 (R), 467154 (R)
Fax: 0532-607367, 623221
Email: krishnamisra@hotmail.com,
kkmisra@yahoo.com

Prof. C.P. Malik
Prof. & Chairperson,
Dept. of Biotechnology,
Guru Jambheshwar University,
Hisar-125 001
Tel: 01662-37608/09- Ext. 242 (O),
25015-16-Ext. 260 (R)
Fax: 0194-421357

Prof. A.M. Shah
Coordinator & Director,
Centre for Research & Development,
University of Kashmir,
Srinagar-190 006, (J&K)
Tel: 0194-429405-Extn. 369,
421656 (R), 422471 (PP)

Prof. B.S. Rajput
Vice Chancellor,
Kumaon University,
Nainital-263001
Uttaranchal
Tel: 05942-35068
Fax: 05942-35576
Email: vc@kumuni.ren.nic.in

M.Sc. Agricultural Biotechnology (2 years)

Prof. P.C. Deka
Dept. of Agricultural Biotechnology,
Assam Agricultural University,
Jorhat-785 013 (Assam)
Tel: 0376-340097, 340101 (O), 340287 (R), 340041 (R)
Fax: 0376-340044, 340001
Email: pcdeka@aau.ren.nic.in

Dr. S. Sadasivam
Director Centre for Plant Molecular Biology,
Tamil Nadu Agricultural University,
Coimbatore-641 003
Tel: 0422-431222, 433890 (O), 451078 (O), 439052 (R)
Fax: 0422-431672
Email: cpmb@hotmail.com

Prof. G.K. Garg
Dept. of Molecular Biology & Genetic Engineering,
College of Basic Sciences & Humanities,
G.B. Pant University of Agri. & Tech.,
Pantnagar-263 145 (Uttaranchal)
Tel: 05944-33374 (O), 33635 (R), 33710 (R)
Fax: 05944-33473
Email: gkgbmb@gbpuat.ernet.in, bmb@gbpuat.ernet.in

Dr. G.S. Dubey
Dean, PGS & Coordinator,
Biotech Centre,
Birsa Agri. University,
Ranchi-834 006 (Jharkhand)
Tel: 0651-455859 (O), 541389 (R), 5211389
Fax: 0651-455850, 304451

Dr. B.M. Singh
Coordinator,
Biotechnology Centre,
Himachal Pradesh Krishi Vishvavidyalaya,
Palampur-176 062 (Himachal Pradesh)
Tel: 01894-30371 (O), 30452 (R)
Fax: 01894-30371, 30511
Email: dcoa@hpkv.hp.nic.in

Dr. S.K. Katiyar
Coordinator,
Biotechnology Centre,
Indira Gandhi Agricultural University,
Raipur-492 012(Chhattisgarh)
Fax: 0771-442131
Email: skatiyar@yahoo.com

Master in Medical Biotechnology (2 years)

Prof. Y. D. Sharma
Coordinator, Department of Biotechnology,
All India Institute of Medical Sciences, Ansari Nagar,
New Delhi-110 029
Tel: 6967045 (dir), 6594609 (dir), 6593617, 6862587 (R), PBX 6864851/4609
Fax: 6852286, 6862663
Email: YDS@aiims.ernet.in

M.Sc. Marine Biotechnology (2 years)

Dr. U.M.X. Sangodkar
Coordinator & Head,
Dept. of Marine Sciences & Biotech.,
Goa University, Teleigao Plateau,
P.O. Bambolim Complex, Goa-403 205
Tel: 0832-PBX-221375, 221345, 221348, 221377 (VC), 417034 (R)
Fax: 0832-224184
Email: umxs@unigoa.ernet.in

M.Tech/M.Sc.(Tech) Biochemical Engineering & Biotechnology (5 years integrated/3 semesters/1.5 year course

Prof. S.C. Kundu
Prof. & Head,
Dept. of Biotechnology,
Indian Institute of Technology,
Kharagpur-721 302
Tel: 03222-82247, 82248, 83764 (work), 83765 (R), 78100 (R)
Fax: 03222-55303, 78433, 82700
Email: kundu@hijli.iitkgp.ernet.in

Prof. G.P. Agarwal
Head, Dept. of Biochemical Engineering and Biotechnology,
Indian Institute of Technology,Hauz Khas,
New Delhi-110 016
Tel: 6596109 (dir), 6591001 (dir), 6581107 (R), 6591851 (R)
Fax: 6868521, 6862037
Email: gopal@dbeb.iitd.ernet.in, gopalpa@hotmail.com

Prof. P. Kaliraj
Director Centre for Biotechnology,
Anna University,
Guindy, Chennai-600 025
Tel: 044-2350299, 2350772, 2351126-Ext. 3565, 4919971 (R)
Fax: 044-2350299
Email: pkaliraj@annauniv.edu, cbiotech@giasmdoi.vsnl.net.in

Prof. J.S. Pai
Coordinator, University Dept. of Chemical Technology (UDCT),
University of Mumbai,
Nathalal Parekh Marg, Matunga,
Mumbai-400 019
Tel: 022-4145616 (O), 6311803 (R)
Fax: 022-4145614
Email: jspai@bpt.udct.ernet.in

Post MD/MS Certificate Course in Medical Biotechnology (1 year)

Prof. Y.D. Sharma
Coordinator (Post MD/MS),
Department of Biotechnology,
All India Institute of Medical Sciences, Ansari Nagar,
New Delhi-110 029
Tel: PBX 6864851/4609, 6862587 (R), 6594609 (dir), 6593617
Fax: 6852286, 6862663

Dr. S. Majumdar
Dept. of Experimental Med. & Biotechnology,
PGI Med. Edu. & Res.,
Chandigarh-160 012
Tel: 0172-540403 (dir), PBX 747586-602
Fax: 744401

Prof. S.S. Aggarwal
Head, Department of Medical Genetics,
Sanjay Gandhi Post Graduate Institute of Medical Sciences,
Raebareli Road,
Lucknow—226014, (U.P.)
Tel: 0522-440732, 0522-440700-extn 2280
Fax:0522-440017,440973
Email: ssa@sgpgi.ac.in

PG Diploma Course in Clinical Biochemistry & Biotechnology (1 year)

Dr. G.B.N. Chainy
Coordinator, International Centre for Applied Biotechnology,
Utkal University, Vani Vihar,
Bhubneshwar-751004
Tel:0674-582805(O), 581503(R)
Fax:0674-509107, 509037
Email: ajay@dte.vsnl.net.in

Registrar, Utkal University
International Centre for Applied Biotechnology,
Utkal University, Vani Vihar,
Bhubneshwar-751 004
Tel: 0674-581387 (O), 581507 (R)
Fax: 0674-509107, 509037
Email: ajay@dte.vsnl.net.in

Vice-Chancellor,
International Centre for Applied Biotechnology,
Utkal University, Vani Vihar,
Bhubneshwar-751 004
Tel: 0674-581850 (O), 581354 (R)
Fax: 0674-581850
Email: ajay@dte.vsnl.net.in

PG Diploma Courses in Molecular & Biochemical Technology (1 year)

Dr. A. Sankara Reddy
Coordinator & Principal,
Sri Venkateswara College,
Benito Juarez Road, Dhaula Kuan,
New Delhi-110 021
Tel:4672196(O),6885565(R)Fax:6118535
Email: asr@ttdsvc.ernet.in

JNU Contact Person

Dr. S. Chandrasekhar
Coordinator Evaluation (Academic)
Administrative Building,
Jawaharlal Nehru University,
New Delhi-110067.
Ph : 6102116 (direct), 6167557 (extn 2012)

List of Research Institutions (CSIR Institutions) at Hyderabad

Dr. Lalji Singh
Director
Centre for Cellular and Molecular Biology (CCMB)
Uppal Road, Hyderabad-500 007
Tel: 7160222
Fax: 7160252

Dr. K.V. Raghavan
Director
Indian Institute of Chemical Technology (IICT)
Uppal Road, Hyderabad-500 007
Tel: 7193030
Fax: 7160387

Dr. Sayed E. Hasnain
Director
Centre for DNA Printing
Nacharam, ECIL Road
Hyderabad- 500 016
Tel: 7150008

Dr. N.P. Sharma
Principle Scientist (Biotechnology)
Directorate of Rice Research
Rajendra Nagar, Hyderabad- 500 030
Tel: 7008921

Dr. S.N. Saha
Acting Director
National Academy of Agricultural Research Management (NAARM)
Rajendra Nagar, Hyderabad-500 030
Tel: 4015394

Dr. Shiva Prasad
Director
National Institute of Nutrition (NIN)
Road No. 38, Main Building
Jamia Osmania, Hyderabad- 500 007
Tel: 7008921

Dr. G.N. Rao
Director
Hyderabad Eye Research Foundation
Road No. 2, Banjara Hills
Hyderabad-500 034
Tel: 3548267

Dr. T. Suryanarayana
Dean
School of Life Sciences
University of Hyderabad
University Campus, Gachibowli-500 046
Tel: 3010500

Prof. T. Ramana
Coordinator
Biotechnology Division
Andhra University
Vishakapatnam-530 003

Prof. P. Hanmath Rao
Head
Department of Genetics
Osmania University Campus
Hyderabad

Dr. Gopal Reddy
Head
Department of Microbiology
Osmania University Campus
Hyderabad

Prof. Maruti Mohan
Head
Department of Biochemistry
Osmania University Campus
Hyderabad

Prof. (Mrs) J. K. Bhalla
Head
Department of Botany
Osmania University Campus
Hyderabad

List of Biotech Firms: AP Government Biotech Policy Document

Shri. S. Dhawan
Chief Executive
Shapoorji Pallonji Biotech Park Pvt. Ltd.
No. A-13, Ground Floor, Street No. 3
Indian Airlines Colony
Begumpet, Secunderbad-500 003
Andhra Pradesh
Tel: 7900893
Email: dhawansuresh@hotmail.com

Deepanwita Chattopadhyay
Chief Executive Officer
ICICI Knowledge Park
Turkapally Village
Shameerpet Mandal
Ranga Reddy District
Hyderabad-500 078
Tel: 3480003, 3480022
Fax: 3480007
Email: deepanwita@icicikp.com

Mr. Vara Prasad Reddy
Managing Director
Shanta Biotech Pvt. Ltd.
Serene Chambers, Road No. 7,
Banjara Hills, Hyderabad-500 034
Tel: 3548507
Fax: 3548476

Managing Director
Bharat Biotech International Ltd.
8-2-248/A-25
Road No. 3, Banjara Hills
Hyderabad-500 034
Tel: 3350794
Fax: 3350344

Dr. Vijay Kumar Datta
Managing Director
Biological E Limited
18/1&3, Azamabad
Hyderabad-500 020
Tel: 7617831
Fax: 7615309

Mr. K.V. Balasubramaniam
Managing Director
Indian Immunologicals Limited
Road No.44, Jubliee Hills
Hyderabad-500 033
Tel: 3544585
Fax: 3544007

Mr. K. Venkataramana
Managing Director
Jupiter Biosciences Ltd.
152, Patel Chambers, II floor
East Nehru Nagar
Secunderabad-500 026
Tel: 7731038
Fax: 7730860

Shri P.V. Bhide, IAS
Chairman and Managing Director
Godavari Fertilizers Limited
50, Vani Nilayam
Sabestian Road-500 003

Dr. Geeta Patel
Godrej Plant Biotech Ltd.
P-15, Jeevan Jyothi
Priya Colony, Kakaguda-500 003
Tel: 7845906

Mr. Mohammad Iqbal
General Manager
Biochemical and Synthetic Products Limited
Post Box No. 2, Sanath Nagar
Hyderabad-500 018
Tel: 3772631
Fax: 3772632

Mr. Prasad Raju
Executive Director
Classic Biotech Exports Limited
133-B, Vengal Rao Nagar
Hyderabad-500 038
Tel: 3816966

Fortune Biotech Limited
B-16, CIE Balanagar
Hyderabad-500 037
Tel: 7063337

Metchnikoff Biosystems Ltd.
6-3-652/5E, Amruta Estates
Somajiguda-500 482
Tel: 3393980

Nuziveedu Seeds Pvt. Ltd.
3-5-821, II floor
Doshi Ford, Basheer Bagh
Hyderabad-500 029
Tel: 3211200
Fax: 6669066

Prabhat Agri Biotech Pvt. Ltd.
3-6-168/7, Hyderguda
Hyderabad-500 029
Tel: 3223689, 3222088, 3220590

Shri P.S.N. Prasad
Sun Floricult Biotech Limited
6-3-788/33, II Floor
Rama Fertility Center Building
Ameerpet, Hyderabad-500 016

Dr. K. Rao
Managing Director
Transgene Biotech Limited
C-44, Madhura Nagar
S.R. Nagar, Ameerpet-500 038
Tel: 3748060

Shri Arun Sawhney
President
Dr. Reddy's Laboratories Ltd.
Bulk Activities
7-1-27, Ameerpet
Hyderabad-500 016
Tel: 3731946, 3731408
Fax: 3734804, 3731955
Email: aruns@drreddys.com

Shri M. Gopalakrishna, IAS (Retd.)
Chairman
Andhra Pradesh State Financial Corporation
5-9-194, Chirag Ali Lane
Hyderabad-500 001
Tel: 3203373
Fax: 3201646
Email: apsfc@hd1.vsnl.net.in

Shri Vikram J.S. Chhatwal
CEO, Apollo Health Street Ltd.
Academic Building
Apollo Hospitals Complex
Jubilee Hills
Hyderabad-500 033
Tel: 3607777, ext. 4447
Fax: 3554353
Email: vikram_chhatwal@appololife.com

ANNEXURE III

SYLLABUS FOR THE B.SC. BIOTECHNOLOGY 3-YEARS COURSE

(Applicable from the Academic Year 2003-2004)
Osmania University, Hyderabad-500 007

I YEAR B.SC.
PAPER I—FUNDAMENTALS OF GENETICS

Unit I—Cell Structure and Cell Division

1.1 Cells as basic units of living systems
1.2 Virus, bacterial, fungal, plant and animal cell (Cell membrane, plasmids)
1.3 Ultrastructure of eukaryotic cell (Cell wall, cell membrane, mitochondria, chloroplast, endoplasmic reticulum, Golgi apparatus, vocuoles)
1.4 Chromosome organisation in Prokaryotes and Eukaryotes
1.5 Structure of specialized chromosomes (Polytene an Lamp Brush)
1.6 Cell Division and Cell Cycle
1.7 Significance of mitosis and meiosis

Unit II—Mechanism of Inheritance

2.1 Mendel's experiments—Factors contributing to success of Mendel's experiments
2.2 Law of segregation—Monohybrid ratio
2.3 Law of Independent assortment—Dihybrids, Trihybrids
2.4 Dominance, partial or incomplete dominance, co-dominance
2.5 Variations in Mendel's laws, Penetrance and expressivity, pleiotropism, epistasis—deviations in F_2 ratios

2.6 Genes and environment—phenocopies
2.7 Linkage and recombination—Discovery of linkage, cytological proof of crossing over
Recombination frequency and map distance
Interference and coincidence
Mitotic crossing over in *Drosophila*
2.8 Mechanism of sex determination—genic balance theory—*Drosophila*
Homogametic and Heterogametic theory
(Human, Mamalian, Birds)
Environmental control of sex determination—Bonellia
2.9 Sex linked inheritance—X-linkage in Haemophilia. Sex limited and sex influenced characters
Y-linkage—Holandric genes

Unit III—Genetic Material

3.1 DNA as the genetic material--Griffiths experiments on transformation in *Streptococcus pneumoniae.* A very, McEleod and McCarty's experiments. Hershey-Chase experiments with radio-labelled T_2 bacteriophage
3.2 RNA as Genetic Material—Tobacco Mosaic Virus
3.3 Structure of DNA—Watson and Crick Model
3.4 Forms of DNA-A, B and Z forms of DNA, Super coiled and related DNA-Role of topoisomerases
3.5 DNA Replication—Models of DNA replication (Semi-conservative, non-conservative models)
Mechanisms of DNA replication—Linear and circular—Rolling circle and theta mechanism of replication
3.6 Reverse transcription

Unit IV—Biostatistics

4.1 Measures of Central values and dispersion. Graphical representation of data. Moments and skewness
4.2 Concept of probability, basic laws and its application to Mendelian segregation. Concept of probability distribution

Binomial and Poisson distributions, Normal distribution and their application to biology

4.3 Concept of sampling and sampling distribution. Concept of test of hypothesis. Applications of t-statistic to biological problems/data: Chi-square statistic applications in biology

4.4 Simple Regression and Correlation. Concept of analysis of variance (one-way classification)

4.5 Introduction to computers: Central Processing Unit (Constants and Variables and Expression, Flow charts). Databases, Surfing on Internet Applications of computers in biology

Practicals

1. Identification of Drosophila stocks (for morphological characters)
2. Monohybrid and dihybrid ratio in Drosophila/maize
3. Genetic interaction and modified dihybrid ratios
4. Problems on Two and Three Point test crossing and gene mapping
5. Estimation of DNA by diphenylamine method and Estimation of RNA by orcinol method
6. Gram staining of bacteria
7. Graphical representation of data (Histograms, frequency polygen, Pie diagram)
8. Fitting of binomial and Poisson distributions

Recommended Books

1. *Biometry* by Sokal and Rohlf W.H. Freeman
2. *Fundamentals of Biometry* by L.N. Balaram (George Allen and Unwil Ltd., London (1972)
3. *Biostatistics* by NTJ Bailey
4. *Genetics* by Garner (Macmillan Press)
5. *An introduction to genetic analysis* by Griffith and others, Freeman and Company
6. *Genetics* by K.B. Ahluwalia [New Age International (P) Ltd.]

7. *Cell Biology* by S.C. Rastogi [New Age International (P) Ltd.]
8. *Statistical Genetics—Principles and Practice* by Prem Narain
9. *Biotechnology* by K.Trehan
10. *Biotechnology-I* by R.S. Setty and G.R.Veena
11. *Biotechnology-II* by R.S. Setty and V. Sreekrishna

II YEAR B.SC.
PAPER II—BIOLOGICAL CHEMISTRY

UNIT I—Biomolecules

1.1 **Carbohydrates:** Importance, classification and properties
1.2 Structure and configuration of Monosaccharides
Monosaccharides: Structure and classification
1.3 Disaccharides—Structure of Sucrose, Lactose, Maltose and Trehalose
Glycosidic linkage and sugars as reducing agents
1.4 Polysaccharides—Storage polysaccharides—Starch and Glycogen
Structural polysaccharides—Cellulose and Chitin
1.5 **Proteins:** Classification and structural features of amino acids
1.6 Stereoisomerism and Zwitter ion properties, Allo forms of amino acids
1.7 Peptide bond characteristics, structure and classification
Different levels of structures of proteins—primary secondary, tertiary and quaternary
1.8 Protein—protein interactions
1.9 **Enzymes**: Classification of enzymes
Kinetics of enzyme catalyzed reactions
1.10 Factors influencing enzymatic reactions
(a) pH (b), Temperature, (c) Substrate concentration, and (d) Enzyme concentration
1.11 Enzyme inhibition—Competitive and non-competitive
1.12 **Lipids**: Fatty acids: Saturated and unsaturated
1.13 Classification of lipids—Saponifiable and non-saponifiable
Triacylglycerols, Phosphoglycerols, Spingolipids, Sterols
Lipid bilayer membranes

Unit II—Intermediary Metabolism

2.1 Glycolysis
2.2 Citric acid cycle
2.3 Gluconeogenesis and its significance
2.4 Mitochondrial electron transport
Chemiosmotic theory of ATP synthesis
2.5 β-Oxidation of fatty acid—Knoop's theory
2.6 Deamination, decarboxylation and transamination reactions of amino acids
2.7 Catabolism of amino acids—phenylalanine and tyrosine (Phenylktonuria and albinism)
2.8 Photosynthesis—Light and dark reactions

Unit III—Biophysical techniques, principles and applications

3.1 Colorimetry and Spectrophotometery—Beer-Lambert's Law
3.2 Microscopy—Light, Inverted, Fluorescent and Electron microscopy
3.3 Chromatography
(a) Paper, (b) Thin Layer, (c) Ion-exchange, (d) Gel-filtration
3.4 Electrophoresis—Paper, Agarose, SDS-PAGE
3.5 Centrifugation
3.6 Dialysis

Unit IV—Membrane Transport

4.1 Facilitated diffusion, passive and active transport
4.2 Carriers, Channels (open and voltage gated)
4.3 Transport of ions
Uniport, symport, antiport
4.4 Na+-K+ pumps in animal cells

Practicals

1. Qualitative tests of sugars, amino acids and lipids
2. Quantitative estimations of protein by Biuret Method
3. Estimation of total sugars by Anthron Method

4. Paper chromatography of amino acids
5. Separation of compounds of TLC
6. Separation of plant pigments on alumina column/paper chromatography
7. Paper electrophoresis of amino acids
8. Enzyme assays—Catalase (any other enzyme)

Recommended Books

1. *Biochemistry* by Dr. U. Satyanarayana
2. *Biochemistry* by J.L. Jain
3. *Biochemistry* by Conn and Stumpf
4. *Biochemistry* by Lehninger
5. *Biochemistry* by Stryer
6. *Biochemistry* by Voet and Voet
7. *Biochemistry* (Jaypee) Vasudevan
8. *Biochemistry* by David Rawn
9. *Practical Biochemistry* by Upadhayay, Wilson & Wilson, Wilson & Wilson & Walker
10. *General Biochemistry* by J.H.Well
11. *Biochemistry* by K.Trehan
12. *Biochemistry* Methods by S. Sadasivam and A. Manickam

For Practicals

Laboratory Manuals by

1. T. Plummer
2. Jayaraman
3. Kanti Mukherjee (3 volumes)

III YEAR B.SC.
PAPER III—MOLECULAR BIOLOGY AND GENETIC ENGINEERING

Unit I—Gene and Genome Organisation

1.1 Nuclear genome organization—Genes and gene numbers—essential and non-essential genes

1.2 Chemical composition of DNA—GC content, C-value and C-value paradox
1.3 Re-association kinetics of DNA—Denaturation and renaturation, dissociation and re-association of DNA-melting temperature (Tm values), Cot curves
1.4 Kinetic classes of DNA—Single copy sequences, and repeated sequences—moderately repeated sequences, highly repeated sequences. Inverted, tandem and palindromic repeats
1.5 Satellite DNA
1.6 Mitochondrial genome organization (e.g.: Human, yeast and plants)
1.7 Chloroplast genome organization—plants
1.8 Organization of eukaryotic genes
1.9 Exons, introns, promoters and terminators
1.10 Gene families and clusters—e.g. Globin gene, histones and ribosomal genes

Unit II—Gene Expression and Regulations

2.1 Transcription
Post-transcriptional modifications (Capping, polyadenylation, splicing and alternate splicing)
2.2 Translation
Genetic code and its features, Single letter notations for amino acids—wobbling
Synthesis of polypeptides—initiation, elongation and termination in prokaryotes and eukaryotes
2.3 Regulation of gene expression in prokaryotes and eukaryotes—Lacoperon, Mating types in yeast

Unit III—Recombinant DNA Technology

3.1 Enzymes used in gene cloning: Restriction endonucleases, Ligases, Phosphatases, Methylases
3.2 Cloning Vehicles—Plasmids, Cosmids, Phage vectors, Shuttle vectors
3.3 Construction of genomic and cDNA libraries

3.4 Identification of cloned genes
3.5 Applications of genetic engineering (Humilin, Somatostatin, Vaccines, Golden rice with Vitamin A)

Unit IV—Basics of Immunology

4.1 Introduction to immune system—Organs and cells of the immune system
4.2 Antigens—physico-chemical characteristics
4.3 Structure of different immunoglobulins and their functions—Primary and secondary antibody responses
4.4 The Major Histocompatibility gene complex and its role in organ transplantation, Generation of antibody diversity

Practicals

1. Extraction of DNA from plant/animal/bacterial cells or tissues
2. Estimation of melting temperature of DNA
3. Immuno-diffusion test
4. Haemagglutisation (e.g. ABO Blood grouping)
5. Problems on restriction mapping
6. Problems on re-association kinetics
7. Viability tests of cells/bacteria (Evans blue test or Trypan blue test)

Recommended Books

1. *Yeast Genetic Engg.* by P.J. Barr, A.J. Brake & P. Valenzuela, Publ., Butterworths
2. *Essential Immunology* by I. Roitt, Publ., Blackwell
3. *Molecular Biology of the Gene* by Watson, Hopkins, Goberts, Steitz and Weiner, Publ., Eenjamin
4. *Cell and Molecular Biology* by Robertis & Robertis, Publ., Waverly
5. *Gene Structure and Expression* by J.D. Howkins, Publ., Cambridge

6. *Genetic Engineering* by R. Williamson, Publ., Cambridge
7. *Test Book of Molecular Biology* by K.S. Sastry, G. Padmanabhan & C. Subramanyan, Publ: Macmillan India
8. *Microbial Genetics* by S.R. Maloy, J.E. Cronan & D. Freifelder, Publ., Jones & Barlett
9. *Principles of Gene Manipulation* by R.W. Old & S.B. Primrose, Publ., Blackwell
10. *Genes* by B. Jewin Publ., Oxford Univ. Press
11. *Molecular Biology & Biotechnology* by H.D. Kumar, Publ., Vikas
12. *Immunology* by G.Reever & I. Todd, Publ., Blackwell
13. *From Genes to Clones* by E.L. Winnacker, Publ., Panima, New Delhi
14. *Methods for General & Molecular Bacteriology,* Ed., P. Gerhard *et al.,* Publ., ASM
15. *Molecular Biotechnology* by G.R. Click and J.J. Pasternak, Publ., Panima
16. *Recombinant DNA* by J.D.Watson *et al.,* Publ., Scientific American Books
17. *Immuno Diagnostics* by S.C. Rastogi, Publ., New Age
18. *Molecular Biology* by D. Freifelder, Publ., Narosa
19. *Genes and Genomes* by Maxine Singer and Paul Berg
20. *Cell and Molecular Biology* by S.C. Rastogi

III YEAR B.SC.
PAPER IV—APPLICATION OF BIOTECHNOLOGY

Unit I—Animal Biotechnology

1.1 Introduction to animal biotechnology
1.2 Importance of livestock production—inbreeding, line breeding, outbreeding and cross-breeding (e.g.: cattle, sheep, swine). Care and management of lab animals (animal environment, housing, management, husbandry)
1.3 Molecular markers and their use in breeding
1.4 *In vitro* fertilization and embryo transfer, artificial insemination, multiple ovulation, fertilization of ova, *in*

vitro culture of embryo, and embryo transfer—control of sex ratio

1.5 Cloning of animals (for economically useful traits such as wool, milk, meat etc.)

1.6 Methods of gene transfer—Micro-injection, Electroporation, Liposome, and viral mediated gene transfer techniques

1.7 Transgenic animal models for studying diseases

1.8 Principles of *Ex vivo* and *In vivo* gene therapy

1.9 Culture of cells and tissues (e.g., stem cells and cellular transplantations for treating diseases)

Unit II—Plant Biotechnology

2.1 Composition of media, Preparation of media and methods of sterilizations

2.2 Role of micronutrients and hormones in morphogenesis

2.3 Meristem culture and production of virus free plants Clonal propagation of plants on a commercial scale

2.4 Production of commercially useful compounds by plant cell culture (Shikonin, alkaloids, food additives)

2.5 Biotransformation by plant cell cultures (Digitoxin, â-methyl digioxin)

2.6 Mass cultivation of cell cultures and process engineering—batch and continuous cultures, Bioreactors

2.7 Applications of plant recombinant DNA technology in agriculture and pharmacy

Unit III—Industrial Biotechnology

3.1 Introduction to microbial biotechnology—Exploitation of microorganisms for economic products

3.2 Primary and secondary metabolic products of microorganisms

3.3 Screening and isolation and preservation of industrial microorganism

3.4 Commercial production of fuels and chemicals by microbial fermentations

3.5 Fermentative production of microbial enzymes (amylases, proteases), and antibiotics
3.6 Fermentative production of foods and dairy products
3.7 Animal cells as bioreactors; characteristics of bioreactors, expression and over production of targeted proteins—human growth harmones—production of α and β-interferons, monoclonal antibodies

Unit IV—Environmental Biotechnology

4.1 Introduction to environmental biotechnology
4.2 Renewable and non-renewable energy resources
4.3 Conventional energy sources and their impact on environment
4.4 Non-Conventional fuels and their impact on environment (biogas, microbial hydrogen, solar energy converters)
4.5 Microbiological quality of milk, food and water
4.6 Microbiological treatment of municipal and industrial effluents
4.7 Microbiological degradation of pesticides and toxic chemicals
4.8 Biopesticides and biofertilizers
4.9 Microbial ore leaching

Practicals

1. Preparation of media, and Initiation of callus cultures from selected plant species
2. Micropropagation of any plant species
3. Production of wine using common yeast
4. Production of hydrogen or biogas using cow/cattle dung
5. Isolation of microbes from soil or industrial effluents
6. Preparation of media and culture of animal cells/tissues
7. Concepts of biosafety methods and bioethics
8. Growth curves of bacteria, Measurement of growth in liquid cultures

Recommended Books

1. *Strategies in Transgenic Animal Sciences* by Glemn, M.M. and James, M. Robl, ASM Press, 2000
2. *Animal Cells as Bioreactors* by Terence Gartoright, Cambridge Univ. Press
3. *Introduction to Veterinary Genetics* by F.W. Nicholas, Oxford University Press
4. *Biotechnology* by H.J. Rehm and G. Reed, Vol. 1-86 VIH Publications, Germany
5. *Guide for the care and use of lab animals,* National Academy Press
6. *Biogas Technology* by B.T. Nijaguna
7. *Biotechnology-I* by R.S. Setty and G.R.Veena
8. *Biotechnology-II* by R.S. Setty and V. Sreekrishna
9. *Introduction of Plant Tissue Culture* by M.K. Razdan (Oxford and IBH Publishing Company, New Delhi)
10. *Introduction to Plant Biotechnology* by H.S. Chawla (Oxford and IBH Publishing Company, New Delhi)
11. *Biotechnology* by K. Trehan
12. *Industrial Microbiology* by L.E. Casida
13. *Food Microbiology* by M.R. Adams and M.O. Moss
14. *Introduction to Biotechnology* by P.K. Gupta
15. *Frontiers of Plant Tissue Culture* by T.A. Thorpe
16. *Plant Tissue Culture—Theory and Practice* by S.S. Bhojwani and M.K. Razdan

BT 101 U: GENETICS

1. Physical Basis of Heredity

1.1 Mendelism: Law of Inheritance
1.2 Gene Interaction and Modification of Mendelian Ratios
1.3 Multiple Alleles
1.4 Multiple Factor Inheritance
1.5 Genes and Environment
1.6 Extra Chromosomal Inheritance

2. Linkage, Recombination and Mapping

2.1 Chromosomal Basis of Inheritance
2.2 Crytological Basis of Crossing Over
2.3 Two Point and Three Point Test Crosses and Gene Mapping
2.4 Mapping of Genes by Tetrad Analysis
2.5 Mitotic and Meiotic Recombination in *Aspergillus*

3. Chromosome Structure, Organisation and Abberations

3.1 Chromosome Morphology, Classification and Karyotyping
3.2 Specialized Chromosomes
3.3 Chromosome Abberations
3.4 Euchromatin and Heterochromatin
3.5 Organisation of Nucleosomes

4. Sex Determination

4.1 Mechanisms of Sex Determination in Animals and Plants
4.2 Sex Differentiation and Development in Humans
4.3 Lyonization and Dosage Compensation
4.4 Sex Linked Disorders in Humans

BT 102 U : BIOCHEMISTRY

1. Structure, Properties and Synthesis of Biomolecules

1.1 Carbohydrates
1.2 Proteins
1.3 Lipids
1.4 Nucleic Acids

2. Enzyme Kinetics

2.1 Catalytic Power of Enzymes
2.2 Classification of Enzymes
2.3 Regulation of Enzyme Activity

2.4 Enzyme Kinetics
2.5 Enzyme Inhibition
2.6 Multienzyme Complexes

3. Bioenergetics

3.1 Laws of Thermodynamics
3.2 High Energy Biomolecules
3.3 Glycolysis
3.4 Tricarboxylic Acid Cycle
3.5 Electron Transport and Oxidative Phosphorylation
3.6 Pentose Phosphate Pathway
3.7 Gluconeogenesis
3.8 Glyoxylate Cycle
3.9 Oxidation of Fatty Acids
3.10 Oxidation of Amino Acids

4. Harmones in Animals and Plants

4.1 Major Endocrine Systems in Animals
4.2 Steroid and Peptide Hormones
4.3 Mechanism of Action
4.4 Cytokinins and Auxins
4.5 Plant Growth Regulators
4.6 Mechanism of Action

BT 102U : BIOCHEMISTRY

1. Chemistry of Biomolecules

1.1 Carbohydrates: Classification, structure (open and ring) of monosaccharides, Reactions of monosaccharides—oxidation, reduction, osazone formation, mutation. Disaccharides—structure and functions—sucrose, lactose, maltose. Polysaccharides: structure and functions of starch, glycogen, chitin and cellulose. Bacterial cell wall polysaccharides.

1.2 Amino acids and proteins: classification of amino acids.

Structure of amino acids. Zwitterions and isoelectric point. Reactions of amino acids—Ninhydrin, Sanger, Edman, and Dansyl Peptide bond, Dipeptides, Polypeptides, Classification of proteins.

1.3 Lipids: Classification, hydrolysis of lipids alkaline and enzymatic. Fatty acids—saturated, unsaturated, essential. Neutral fats, Rancidity Phosphotipids, Structure and biological functions. Steroids.

1.4 Nucleic acids: Purines, pyrimidines, nucleosides, nucleotides. DNA-types replication, properties—denaturation hyperchromicity, salient features of Watson and Crick model of DNA, RNA types and function.

2.0 Enzymology

2.1 Introduction of enzymes—apoenzyme, coenzyme, prosthetic group. Cofactors, units of activity, factors effecting enzyme action.

2.2 Classification of enzymes

2.3 Isoenzymes and Zymogens

2.4 Enzyme kinetics: Michaells-Mention equation (no derivation), significance of Km and Vmax.

2.5 Enzyme inhibition; feedback, competitive, noncompetitive and allosteric inhibition, Lineweaver-Burk plats

2.6 Multienzyme complexes—pyruvate dehydrogenase

3.0 Bioenergetics and Metabolism

3.1 Biological oxidation, free energy concept. Free energy changes and high energy compounds. Redox potentials. Biological redox systems

3.2 Electron transport chain and oxidative phosphorylation

3.3 Gycolysis and TCA cycle. Reactions and energetics. Substrate level phosphorylation

3.4 Glyoxylate cycle

3.5 Pentose phosphate pathway and its physiological significance

3.6 β-Oxidation of fatty acids and its energetic

3.7 Oxidation of amino acids—L-amino oxidase. Be-PO_4 dependent reactions
3.8 Biosynthesis of fatty acids
3.9 Gluconeogenesis

4.0 Animal and Plant Hormones

4.1 Organization of endocrine system. Classification of hormones
4.2 Brief account of (structure and functions) thyroid, parathyroid, pancreatic, adrenal, pituitary and gonadal hormones. Menstrucal cycle—Oral contraceptive drugs
4.3 Outline of endocrine disorders
4.4 Plant hormones—cytokinins and auxins. Mechanism of action

BT 152 U: Methods of Microbiology and Biochemistry

5.0 Determination of maximum absorption of compounds. Absorption spectra of protein and nucleic acid. Buffer preparation. Estimation of protein by Biuret and Lowry method (Falin's method)
6.0 Separation of amino acids and carbohydrates by paper chromatography. PAGE (demonstration only)
7.0 Estimation of DNA and RNA by diphenylamine and orcinol methods
8.0 Determination of inorganic phosphorus by Fiske and Subba Raw's procedure. Vitamin C estimation by dichlorophenol indophenol method
9.0 Enzyme assays. Amylase (salivary), Urease (Jack bean meal/ Horse gram). Specific activity determination. Influence of pH, temperature and substrate concentration on the activity of any one enzyme.

BT 103 U: MICROBIOLOGY

1. General Characters and Culturing of Microbes

1.1 Bacteria

1.2 Algae
1.3 Fungi
1.4 Viruses

2. Microbial Growth and Physiology

2.1 Nutritional Requiremcnts of Microbes
2.2 Bacterial Growth
2.3 Kinetics of Viral infection
2.4 Lytic Cycle and Lysogeny

3. Recombination in Bacterial and Viruses

3.1 Identification of Mutant Strains
3.2 Transformation
3.3 Transduction
3.4 Conjugation

4. Gene Regulation in Prokaryotes

4.1 Regulation of Lactose Utilization
4.2 Regulation of Tryptophan Biosynthesis

BT 104 U: BIOMETRY

1. Probability Theory and Distribution

1.1 Exclusive and Independent Events, Permutations and Combinations
1.2 Laws of Probability and their use in Biology
1.3 Probability Distribution and Properties

2. Statistical Inference and Qualitative and Quantitative Variables

2.1 Random and Non-Random Sampling
2.2 Estimation and Confidence Interval

2.3 Test of Hypothesis and Level of Significance for Chi Square Test, Linkage and Heterogienity
2.4 Large and Small and Sample Test

3. Analysis of Variance and Co-Variance

3.1 One-way ANOVA and F-test
3.2 Two-way ANOVA
3.3 Scattered Diagrams, Co-variance, Correlation and Regression Coefficients
3.4 Growth Curves
3.5 Multiple Linear Regression and Correlation Coefficients

4. Computer Programming and Applications

4.1 Computer Languages
4.2 Basic Principals in Programming
4.3 Applications in Biotechnology

BT 201 U: CELL BIOLOGY

1. Cell Structure

1.1 Prokaryotic Cell
1.2 Eukaryotic Cell
1.3 Ultrastructure and Biogenesis of Organelles

2. Membranes and Transport

2.1 Ultra Structure of Membranes
2.2 Passive Transport
2.3 Active Transport
2.4 Ion Channels

3. Signal Transduction

BT 204 U: IMMUNOLOGY

1. Overview of Immune Response

1.1 Innate and Acquired Immunity
1.2 Antigens, Haptens and Adjuvants
1.3 Immune Systems
1.4 Immunoglobulins
1.5 Antigen and Antibody Interactions

2. Genetics of Immunoglobulins

2.1 Organisation of Immunoglobulin genes
2.2 Generation of Antibody Diversity
2.3 Clonal Selection

3. Immune Responses

3.1 Primary and Secondary Antibody Responses
3.2 Response to Haptens
3.3 Cell Mediated Immunity
3.4 Immune Response Genes and Control of Macrophage Interactions with Lymphocytes
3.5 MHC Molecules and their role in Immune Regulation
3.6 T-Cell Receptors Role in Regulation of Antibody Synthesis
3.7 Complement Systems

4. Histocompatability Systems

4.1 Transplantation Immunity and Graft Rejection
4.2 Major Histocompatability Complex in Antigen Presentation
4.3 Auto Immune Diseases

BT 201U: CELL BIOLOGY

1. Cell Structure

1.1 Prokaryotic Cell
1.2 Eukaryotic Cell

1.3 Ultrastructure and Biogenesis of Organelles

2. Membranes and Transport

2.1 Ultrastructure of Membranes
2.2 Passive Transport
2.3 Active Transport
2.4 Ion Channels

3. Signal Transduction

3.1 Hormones and Signal Transduction Pathways
3.2 Intracellular Second Messengers
3.3 GTP Binding Proteins
3.4 Protein Kinases
3.5 Protein Modules in Signal Transduction

4. Cell Cycle and Division

4.1 Phases of Cell Cycle
4.2 Methods of Cell Synchronization
4.3 Regulation of Cell Cycle, CDE Mutants
4.4 Cell Division
4.5 Deregulated Cell Division and Cancer.

BT 202U: MOLECULAR BIOLOGY-1

1. Genetic Material

1.1 DNA as Genetic Material
1.2 RNA as Genetic Material
1.3 Forms of DNA
1.4 Replication of linear and circular DNA

2. DNA Damage and Repair

2.1 Molecular Mechanism of Mutations
2.2 Mechanisms of DNA Repair

3. Expression of Genetic Information

3.1 Transcription of DNA
3.2 Genetic Code
3.3 Translation of RNA

4. Plasmids and IS Elements

4.1 Classification, Properties and Significance of Plasmids
4.2 IS Elements and Transposons

BT 203 U: MOLECULAR BIOLOGY-II

1. Organisation of Nuclear and Organellar Genomes

1.1 Genome Size and C value Paradox
1.2 Reassociation kinetics
1.3 Tm Values
1.4 Satellite DNA
1.5 Mitocondrial Genome
1.6 Chloroplast Genome

2. Eukaryotic Genes and their Expression

2.1 Special features of Eukaryotic Genes
2.2 Organisation of Eukaryotic Genes
2.3 Transcription and Processing of r-RNA
2.4 Transcription and Processing of t-RNA
2.5 Transcription and Processing of m-RNA
2.6 Regulation of Gene Expression

3. Recombination of DNA

3.1 Rearrangement of DNA
3.2 Recombination pathways involving recogenes
3.3 Site Specific Recombination

4. Eukaryotic Transposable Elements

4.1 Discovery of Transposable Elements
4.2 Molecular Structure and Transposition of AC/DS System
4.3 P Element and Hybrid dysgenesis
4.4 TY Elements
4.5 Transposon Tagging

BT 401 U: MEDICAL BIOTECHNOLOGY

1. Biotechnological Approaches for Diagnosis and Treatment of Infectious Diseases

1.1 Epidemiology of Tropical Diseases with Special reference to Malaria, Cholera, Leprosy, Tuberculosis and Hepatitis
1.2 Probes for Diagnosis
1.3 Prevention and Control of Infection

2. Diagnosis of Genetic Diseases

2.1 Metabolic and Chromosomal Disorders
2.2 Heterozygote Identification
2.3 Prenatal Diagnosis
2.4 Neonatal Screening

3. Gene Therapy

3.1 Methods of Gene therapy
3.2 Gene Targeting
3.3 Prospects for Germline Gene therapy
3.4 DNA Based Drugs

4. DNA Fingerprinting and its Applications

4.1 DNA Based Markers
4.2 Micro Array Technology
4.3 Applications

BT 402 U: PLANT BIOTECHNOLOGY

1. Development of Aseptic Cultures and Mass Propagation of Plants

1.1 Initiation and Establishment of aseptic cultures
1.2 Study of Growth curves
1.3 Batch and Continuous Cultures
1.4 Role of Plant Growth Regulators
1.5 Morphogenetic Pathways
1.6 Micropropagation
1.7 Production of Virus free Plants
1.8 Cryopreservation and Conservation of Germplasm

2. *In Vitro* Methods of Crop Improvement and Production of Transgenics

2.1 Isolation of Mutants/Variants
2.2 Another Culture and Production of Haploids/dihaploids
2.3 Isolation, Culture and Plant Regeneration from Protoplasts
2.4 Somaclonal variation
2.5 Somatic hybridization and Production of Hybrids/Cybrids
2.6 Methods of Genetic Transformation
2.7 Candidate Genes for Production of Transgenics
2.8 Prospects and problems of transgenics

3. Production of Commercially Useful Compounds Using Plant Cell/Organ Culture

3.1 Mass cultivation of plant cells/organs indifferent types of bioreactors
3.2 Factors influencing commercial production of secondary metabolites *in vitro*
3.3 Immobilization, elicitor treatment, precursor feeding for yield enhancement
3.4 Biotransformation

4. Industrial Applications of Plant Biotechnology

4.1 Pharmaceuticals
4.2 Food Additives
4.3 Speciality Chemicals
4.4 Quality Oils
4.5 Molecular Farming
4.6 Edible Vaccines

BT 403 U: ENVIRONMENTAL BIOTECHNOLOGY

1. Pollutants and Ecosystems

1.1 Classification of Pollutants
1.2 Effects on the Environment
1.3 An Overview of Industrial and Urban Sewerage
1.4 Current Methods of Disposal
1.5 Monitoring of Environmental Pollutants

2. Bioremediation and Biodegradation

2.1 Leaching and Microbial Mining
2.2 Indicator Plants and Bioprospecting
2.3 Bioremediation of Waste water, Industrial Effluents and Soils
2.4 Biodegradation of Natural Substances, Xenobiotics, Herbicides and Pesticides

3. Energy Recycling

3.1 Hydrogen Evolving Bacteria
3.2 Microbial Degradation of Cellulose and Lignocellulose
3.3 Methanogensis
3.4 Plant Based Fuels

4. Biofertilizers and Biopesticides

4.1 Rhizobium
4.2 Bluegreen algae
4.3 Micorrhiza
4.4 Azolla
4.5 Bacillus thuringensis
4.6 Nuclear Polyhydrosis Virus
4.7 Botanical Pesticides

BT 404 U: ANIMAL BIOTECHNOLOGY

1. Reproductive Systems and Animal Improvement

1.1 Physiological and Cellular Basis of Development
1.2 Hormones and Regulation of Development
1.3 Breeding Selected Traits and into Live Stock Herds

2. *In vitro* Culture of Cells and Tissues

2.1 Maintenance of Cell Cultures
2.2 Properties of Cell Lines
2.3 Monoclonal Antibodies
2.4 Vaccines and Hormones Production
2.5 *In vitro* Production of Tissues and Organs

3. Animal Models for Human Diseases

3.1 Model Laboratory Animals
3.2 Mouse Model for Thalasseamia
3.3 Immuno Deficiency Disease in Mammals

4. Biotechnology Applications

4.1 *In vitro* Fertilization and Embryo Transfer
4.2 Cloning of Mammals
4.3 Transgenic Animals

LABORATORY (PRACTICALS)

BT 151 U: Methods of Genetic Analysis and Biometry

1. Monohybrid and Dihybrid Ratios
2. Modified Dihybrid Ratios
3. Linkage Analysis and Gene Mapping in Eukaryotes
4. Graphical Representations and Calculation of Descriptive Measures
5. Fitting of Bionomial, Poisson and Normal Distributions
6. Chi-Square Test and Goodness of Fit, Contingency and Heterogenity
7. Large and Small Sample Tests
8. Correlation and Regression
9. One-way and Two-way ANOVA

BT 152 U: Methods of Microbiology and Biochemistry

1. Staining Techniques in Bacteria
2. Media and Sterilization Procedures
3. Development of Pure Cultures
4. Bacterial Growth Curves
5. Phage Titration
6. Preparation of Buffers
7. Separation of Aminoacids by Chromatography
8. Estimation of Proteins and Nuclei Acids
9. Separation of Proteins by PAGE
10. Enzyme assays

BT 251U: Methods of Microbiology and Biochemistry

1. Isolation of Genomic DNA
2. Isolation of RNA
3. Size Determination of DNA
4. Reassociation Kinetics of DNA

BT 252 U: Methods of Cell Biology and Immunology

1. Preparation of Mitotic and Meiotic Chromosomes
2. Microhaemoagglutination
3. Immunodiffusion assay
4. Assessment of Leucocyte Migration inhibition
5. Histological Analysis of Tunmonr and normal tissues
6. Ionchannels

BT-LAB-V

1. Isolation of plasmids
2. Bacterial Transformation
3. Cloning and selection of recombinants
4. Characterization and expression of recombinant clones
5. Production of Alcohol/Organic acids/Antibiotics in ferments
6. Methods of product recovery
7. Sequence analysis using Internet resources

BT-LAB-VI

1. PCR Technology for identification of human diseases
2. Productions of Secondary metabolition using plant cell cultures
3. Measurement of environment pollutants
4. Microbiological water quality testing
5. Culturing of Mammalian cells

LABORATORY (PRACTICALS)

BT 351 U: Methods of Genetic Engineering and Bio-informatics

1. Isolation of plasmids
2. Bacterial Transformation
3. Cloning
4. Selection of recombinants
5. Sequence Analysis using Internet Resources

BT 352 U: Methods of Industrial Microbiology and Process Engineering

1. Production of Alcohol in fermenters
2. Production of Antibiotics
3. Organic acids
4. Methods of product recovery

BT 353 U: Methods of Medical and Animal Biotechnology

1. Analysis and Mapping of Human genes and geneotypes by molecular markers
2. PCR technology for identifying human metabolic disorders/ diseases
3. Mutation detection (Haemoglobinopathies etc.)
4. Culturing of Mammalian cells
5. Single cell gel electrophoresis to assay DNA damage

BT 354 U: Methods of Plant and Environmental Biotechnology

1. Production of Secondary metabolites using plant cell cultures
2. Biotransformation using plant cell/tissue cultures
3. Production of industrially useful compounds by cell/tissue immobilization/Elicitors
4. Assay of Environmental pollution and measurement of pollutants
5. Microbial water quality testing.

JAWAHARLAL NEHRU TECHNOLOGY UNIVERSITY
HYDERABAD
COURSE ON BIO-TECHNOLOGY
FIRST YEAR

Subject Code	*Subject*	*T*	*P*	*C*
BT 1001	English	3		6
BT 1002	Mathematics—1	3		6
BT 1003	Applied Biology	3		6
BT 1004	Computer & Information Technology	3		6
BT 1005	C & Data Structures	3		6
BT 1006	Electrical & Electronics	3		6
BT 1007	Computer Programming Lab		6	8
BT 1008	EEE Lab		3	4
BT 1009	Engineering Drawing Practice		3	4
BT 1010	Basic WS		3	4
	TOTAL	**18**	**15**	**56**

T: Theory periods per week
P: Practical/Drawing periods per week
C: Total Credits for the subject

SECOND YEAR : I-SEMESTER

Subject Code	*Subject*	*T*	*P*	*C*
BT 2101	Cell Biology	4	-	4
BT 2102	Micro Biology	4	-	4
BT 2103	Bio Organic Chemistry	4	-	4
BT 2104	Bio Chemistry	4	-	4
BT 2105	Chemical and Bio Thermodynamics	4	-	4
BT 2106	Genetics	4	-	4
BT 2107	Bio Organic Chemistry Lab	-	3	2
BT 2108	Bio Chemistry Lab	-	3	2
	TOTAL	**24**	**6**	**28**

SECOND YEAR : II-SEMESTER

Subject Code	*Subject*	*T*	*P*	*C*
BT 2201	Probability & Statistics	4	-	4
BT 2202	Basic Industrial Bio Technology	4	-	4
BT 2203	Bio Process Engineering I	4	-	4
BT 2204	Enzyme Engineering & Technology	4	-	4
BT 2205	Instrumental Methods of Analysis	4	-	4
BT 2206	Molecular Biology	-	3	2
BT 2207	Micro Biology Lab	-	3	2
BT 2208	Instrumental Methods of Analysis Lab.	‘	3	2
	TOTAL	**24**	**6**	**28**

T : Theory periods per week.
P : Practical/Drawing periods per week.
C: Total Credits for the subject.

THIRD YEAR : I-SEMESTER

Subject Code	*Subject*	*T*	*P*	*C*
BT 3101	Mass Transfer & Separation	4	-	4
BT 3102	Genetic Engineering	4	-	4
BT 3103	Biochemical Engineering	4	-	4
BT 3104	Plant Bio Technology	4	-	4
BT 3105	Environmental Bio Technology	4	-	4
BT 3106	Bio Ethics	4	-	4
BT 3107	Molecular Biology Lab	-	3	2
BT 3108	Bio Process Lab	-	3	2
	TOTAL	**24**	**6**	**28**

THIRD YEAR : II-SEMESTER

Subject Code	*Subject*	*T*	*P*	*C*
BT 3201	Instrumentation and Process Control	4	..	4
BT 3202	Analytical Techniques in Bio Technology	4	-	4
BT 3203	Bio Informatics	4	-	4
BT 3204	Bio Processing Engineering II	4	-	4
BT 3205	Immunology	4	-	4
BT 3206	Protein Engineering	4	-	4
BT 3207	Bio Process Engineering Lab-II		3	2
BT 3208	Genetic Engineering Lab		3	2
	TOTAL	**24**	**6**	**28**

T : Theory periods per week.
P : Practical/Drawing periods per week
C: Total Credits for the subject

FOURTH YEAR : I-SEMESTER

Subject Code	*Subject*	*T*	*P*	*C*
BT 4101	Genomics & Proteomics	4	-	4
BT 4102	Down Stream Processing	4	-	4
BT 4103	Molecular Modelling & Drug Design	4	-	4
BT 4104	Bio Process Econimics & Plant Design	4	-	4
BT 4105	Elective-1	4	-	4
BT 4106	Elective-II	4	-	4
BT 4107	Down Stream Processing Lab	-	3	2
BT 4108	Immunology Lab.	-	3	2
	TOTAL	**24**	**6**	**28**

Elective—I (BT 4105)
1. Cancer Biology
2. Bio-Pharmaceutical Technology
3. Molecular Pathogenics.

Elective—II (BT 4106)
1. Creativity, Innovation & New Product Development
2. Biological Spectroscopy
3. Metabolic Engineering

FOURTH YEAR : II-SEMESTER

Subject code	Subject	T	P	C
BT 4201	Elective-III	4	-	4
BT 4202	Elective-IV	4	-	4
BT 4203	Project Work & Seminar	-	-	8
	TOTAL	8		16

Executive-III (BT 4201)
1. Chromatographic Separations
2. Food Science & Technology
3. Developmental Biology

Elective-IV (BT 4202)
1. Bio-Physics
2. Neuro Biology & Cognitive Sciences
3. Bio Diversity, IPR & Management of BT

T : Theory periods per week
P : Practical/Drawing periods per week
C : Total Credits for the subject

MADRAS UNIVERSITY
M.SC. DEGREE COURSE IN BIOTECHNOLOGY
2 YEARS SEMESTER SYSTEM
WITH CREDITS REGULATIONS

1. Eligibility for Admission

A candidate with Bachelor's Degree in Science in the disciplines of Biology, Botany, Zoology, Biotechnology, Microbiology and Chemistry, Biochemistry, Physics, Agriculture, BE/B.Tech (Biotech), B.V.Sc., MBBS, BDS from this University or an examination of some other University accepted by the Syndicate of this University as equivalent thereto shall be permitted to appear and qualify for the M.Sc. Degree examination of University after a course of two academic years in an affiliated college of this University.

2. Duration of the Course

The duration of the Course is Two Academic years consisting of four semesters. In order to be eligible for the award of the degree, the candidate should have successfully completed the course within Three years reckoned from the date of enrolment for the first semester of the course.

3. Structure of the Course

The course is organized on semester basis with a total of four semesters with 72 credits. In each semester, there are four theory papers (I, II and III semesters 16 hrs/week; and in the fourth semester 14 hrs/week) and one practical course with 14 hrs project work per week.

Independent practical shall be held under each course. For examination purpose, a comprehensive 6 hrs practical examination be held for each semester, covering different courses offered during that semester. It is recommended that the practical training be organized as an exercise rather that simple demonstration. The students must actually perform the experiments.

4. Course of Study and Scheme of Examination

FIRST YEAR

Subject	*Credits*	*Lecture Hrs/Week*	*Practical Hrs/week*	*Exam Hrs.*	
Semester II				*Theory*	*Practical*
Paper-1 Biochemistry and Biomolecules	3	4	0	3	0
Paper-2 Molecular Genetics	3	4	0	3	0
Paper-3 Molecular Cell Biology	4	4	0	3	0
Paper-4 Microbiology	3	4	0	3	6
Paper-5 Practical-I Biochemistry and Biomolecules, Molecular Genetics, Molecular Cell Biology	5	0	14	0	6
Total	18	16	14	12	6

Subject	*Credits*	*Lecture Hrs/Week*	*Practical Hrs/week*	*Exam Hrs.*	
Semester II				*Theory*	*Practical*
Paper-6 Biophysics, Biostatistics an computer applications	3	4	0	3	0
Paper-7 Microbial Bio-process technology	3	4	0	3	0
Paper-8 Animal Cell Biotechnology	3	4	0	3	0
Paper-9 Plant Biotechnology	4	4	0	3	6
Paper-10 Animal Cell Biotechnology Microbial Bio-process technology, Plant Biochemistry	5	0	14	0	6
Total	18	16	14	12	6

SCHEME OF PRACTICAL EXAMINATION

Practical : (6 hrs; 40 marks; 30 + 5 Records + 5 Viva voce)
Biochemistry and Biomolecules, Molecular Genetics and Molecular Cell Biology
Practical II (6 hrs; 40 marks; 30+5 Record + Viva voce)

Animal Cell Biotechnology Microbial Bio-process Technology, Plant Biochemistry.

Subject	*Credits*	*Lecture Hrs/Week*	*Practical Hrs/week*	*Exam Hrs.*	
Semester III				*Theory*	*Practical*
Paper-11 Cloning Vectors	3	4	0	3	0
Paper-12 Genetic Engineering	4	4	0	3	0
Paper-13 Engineering	3	4	0	3	0
Paper-14 Enzyme Technology	3	4	0	3	0
Paper-15 Practical III-Genetic Engineering, Immuno-technology, Enzyme Technology	5	0	14	0	6
Total	18	16	14	12	6

Subject	*Credits*	*Lecture Hrs/Week*	*Practical Hrs/week*	*Exam Hrs.*	
Semester IV				*Theory*	*Practical*
Paper-16 Tissue Engineering	3	4	0	3	0
Paper-17 Genomics and Proteomics	3	4	0	3	0
Paper-18 Environmental Biotechnology	3	4	0	3	0
Paper-19 Bioethics, Biosafety, IPR, Human Rights and Social Issues	2	2	0	3	0
Paper-20 Practical IV-Environmental Biotechnology	2	0	2	-	6
Dissertation and Viva voce	5	-	14	-	Viva voce
Total	18	14	16	12	6

SCHEME OF PRACTICAL EXAMINATION

Practical III (6 hrs; 40 marks; 30+5 Records+5 Viva voce)
Genetic Engineering, Immunotechnology, Enzyme Technology

Practical IV (6 hrs.; 40 marks; 30+5 Records + 5 Viva voce)
Environmental Biotechnology

FIRST YEAR
SCHEME OF EXAMINATION OF THEORY PAPERS

I Semester		
Paper-1 Biochemistry and Biomolecules	3 hrs	100 marks
Paper-2 Molecular Genetics	3 hrs	100 marks
Paper-3 Molecular Cell Biology	3 hrs	100 marks
Paper-4 Microbiology	3 hrs	100 marks
Paper-5 Practical-I Biochemistry and Biomolecules, Molecular Genetics Molecular Cell Biology.	6 hrs.	50 marks

II Semester		
Paper-6 Biophysics, Biostatistics and Computer Application	3 hrs	100 marks
Paper-7 Microbial Bio-process technology	3 hrs	100 marks
Paper-8 Animal Cell Biotechnology	3 hrs	100 marks
Paper-9 Plant Biotechnology	3 hrs	100 marks
Paper-10 Practical-II Animal Cell Biotechnology, Microbial Bio-process Technology, Plant Biotechnology	6 hrs	50 marks

SECOND YEAR
SCHEME OF EXAMINATION OF THEORY AND PAPERS

III Semester		
Paper-11 Cloning Vector	3 hrs	100 marks
Paper-12 Genetic Engineering	3 hrs	100 marks
Paper-13 Immunotechnology	3 hrs	100 marks
Paper-14 Enzyme Technology	3 hrs	100 marks
Paper-15 Practical-III Genetic Engineering, Immunotechnology, Enzyme Technology	6 hrs	50 marks

IV Semester		
Paper-16 Tissue Engineering	3 hrs	100 marks
Paper-17 Genomics and Protenomics	3 hrs	100 marks
Paper-18 Environmental biotechnology	3 hrs	100 marks
Paper-19 Bioethics, Biosafety, IPR, Human rights and social issues	3 hrs	100 marks
Paper-20 Practical-IV Environmental Biotechnology	6 hrs	50 marks
Dissertation and Viva voce	Viva voce	200 marks

5. Passing Requirement

Marks system follows the University regulation. Each theory course carries a maximum of 100 marks. A practical course carries a maximum of 50 marks.

For each theory or practical course, 20 per cent of the total marks is allotted to internal assessment 80 per cent for university examination.

The internal assessment for each course will be carried out by the course instructors. This will consist of at least two mid-term tests (or assignments) and one comprehensive examination at the end of the semester. At the end of each test, the marks will be announced to the students and entered in the register.

A candidate will be declared to have passed in any paper (including practical and project work) if he/she secures not less than 50 per cent of the total marks (the Continuous Internal Assessment and the end Semester University Examination, put together) provided a minimum of 35 out of 80 marks is secured in the University Examination. Tabulation of Final results : The marks obtained in each course internal and external will be entered separately

The duration of examination for each theory paper will be 3 hours and the duration of practical examination for each paper will be 6 hours.

The conduct of supplementary examination will follow the University regulations for post-graduate courses.

6. Project Evaluation

Project : Project work should be carried out as an individual project and actual benchwork. He/she should have passed all the prescribed papers as in the syllabus for the award of the degree. It will begin from IIIrd Semester and will continue through the IVth Semester. The project report will be submitted at the end of IVth semester and evaluated.

For the conduct of the End Semester Examination and Evaluation of Project work the University will appoint external Examiners.

The project dissertation carries a total of 200 marks and evaluation will be carried out by both internal and external evaluators. The average will be considered. The viva voce examination is part of assertation which carries marks as specified below.

The assignment of marks for Project is as follows :

Continuous Internal Assessment	50 marks
Project Work	125 marks
Viva voce	25 marks

CLASSIFICATION OF SUCCESSFUL CANDIDATES

Results will be declared after every University examination in each semester and the marks obtained by the candidate will be forwarded to them through the head of Institutions.

A candidate who has passed all the subjects of examination shall be declared to have passed in first class if he/she secures not less than 60 per cent in the aggregate of all the subjects put together taking both the University and sessional marks.

A candidate who has passed all the subjects of examination shall be declared to have passed in First class with distinction if he/she secures 75 per cent or more than 75 per cent in the aggregate of all the subjects put together taking both the University and sessional marks.

Percentage of Marks	*Class*
75% and above	First Class with Distinction
60% and above but below 75%	First Class
50% and above but below 60%	Second Class

Only those candidates who have passed all the papers including the practical and project work in the first appearance are considered for ranking.

7. Procedure in the Event Failure

1. If a candidate fails in a particular subject (other than project work) he/she appears for the University Examination in that subject in the subsequent semesters and obtain pass marks.
2. In the event of failure in project work the candidates will re-register for the project work and redo the project work in the subsequent semester and resubmit the dissertation afresh for evaluation. The continuous internal assessment marks will be allotted freshly in this case.

Revision of Regulation of Curriculum

The University may from time to time revise or change or amend the regulations scheme of examinations subject of study and the syllabi.

Question paper pattern for M.Sc. Biotechnology degree course for each semester will be as follows:

8. For Theory Paper Subjects

PATTERN OF QUESTION PAPER
PART A (50 WORDS)

Objective questions of definition of 2 marks covering all unit of the syllabus (No choice which is give) 5×4 = 20 Marks

PART B (250 WORDS)

Paragraph questions (Totally ten questions) of 6 marks to be answered choosing one each from each unit following either or pattern 5×8 = 40 Marks

PART C (500 WORDS)

Give essay questions of 10 marks to be answered choosing one from each unit, following either or pattern 5×20 = 100 Marks

UNIVERSITY OF MADRAS
M.SC. DEGREE COURSE IN BIOTECHNOLOGY
(2 YEARS) SEMESTER SYSTEM WITH
CREDITS SYLLABUS

Effective from the Academic Year—2003-2004 and thereafter

PAPER 1
BIOCHEMISTRY AND BIOMOLECULES

Unit-I

Chemical foundation of biology pH, Pk acid, bases, weak bonds, convalent bonds, Principles of thermodynamics, classes of organic compounds and functional groups—atomic and molecular dimensions space filling and ball and stick models.

Unit-II

Definition, nomenclature, classification, structure, chemistry and properties of carbohydrates; lipids; amino acids peptides and proteins; pyrimidines, nucleotides, poly-necleotides; Methods for isolation and characterization of proteins; chemical synthesis of peptides; study of specific proteins like hemoglobin, myoglobin and plasma proteins—classification of prophymins, their structure and properties; structure of metalloporphyris—haeme and chlorophyll—Vitamins and Hormones.

Unit-III

Principles of Bio-energetic; Metabolism of carbohydrates, fats, proteins, purines and pyrimidines—their biosynthesis and degradation; mechanism of oxidative phosphorylation and its inhibitors and photophosphorylation, urea cycle, hormonal regulation of mammalian metabolism.

Unit-IV

Prostaglandins, teukoterines, thermoboxanes; interferon's and interleukins; antibodies; alkaloids; plant and animal pigments, Separation methods—chromatography—paper, absorption, ion-exchange, thin layer, gas, reverse phase and affinity chromatography, high performance; gelfiltration.

Unit-V

Electrophoreses—moving boundary, paper starch, agarose and polycrylamide gel electrophoresis (PAGE & SDS PAGE); disc and slab gel electrophoresis; ID and 2D electrophoresis; immunoelectrophoresis, high voltage electrophoresis, isoelectric focusing, Isolation methods—tissue slice technique; tissue homogenate cell fractionation by differential centrifugation; ultra-centrifugation; density gradient centrifugation.

REFERENCES

1. L. Stryer, 1999, *Biochemistry,* 4th edition, W.H. Freeman & Co., New York.
2. R. Rapley & J.M. Walker, 1998, *Molecular Biomethods Handbooks,* Humana Press.
3. *Principles of Biochemistry,* by A.L. Lehninger.
4. G.L. Zubay, 1998, *Biochemistry,* 4th edition, McGraw-Hill.
5. Harper's *Biochemistry.*
6. *Biochemistry* by D.Voet and J.G.Voet.

PAPER 2
MOLECULAR GENETICS

Unit-I

Gene as a unit of mutation and recombination.

Identification of DNA as a genetic material Mutation; Molecular nature, chemical mutagenesis by nitrous acid, hydroxylamine, alkylation agents, intercalators and physical mutation by UV, origin of spontaneous mutation and its control,

DNA damage and repair: Chemical and physical agents and cross linkers—Mechanism of repair; Photo reactivation, excision repair, recommendational repair—The SOS and adaptive responses and their regulation—Heat shock response.

Parasexual processes in bacteria : transformation, transduction and conjugal gene transfer; their phenomena, mechanism and application.

Unit-II

Fine structure of the gene.

Recombination, controls, models and explanation—Gene as the unit of expression—Colineartiy of the gene and polypeptide—Elucidation of the genetic code—Wobble base pairing—Suppression of nonsense, missense and frame shift mutation—Regulation of gene expression—The Operon concept positive negative and attenuation control—Control sequences: promoter, operator, terminator and attenuator.

Unit-III

Extra chromosomal heredity: biology of plasmids, their discovery, types and the structure of F, RTH, col factors and Ti—Replication and partitioning—Incompatibility and copy number control—natural and artificial plasmid transfers and their applications.

Unit-IV

Transposable genetic elements : Discovery—Early experiments of McClintockin Maize—Insertion sequence in prokaryotes—Complex transposons (ex. Tn10, Tn5, Tn9 and Tn3)—Mechanisms, control, consequences and application of transposition by simple and complex elements.

Unit-V

Genetics of eukaryotes : gene linkage and chromosome mapping—

crossing over three point cross—tetrad analysis—complementation—Organisation of chromosomes and specialized chromosomes—Chromosome abnormalities—Quantitative inheritance—Population genetics—Development genetics using Drosophia as a model system—somatic gene analysis.

REFERENCES

1. *Genetics Schaum's Otutline Series 4e* by Susan Elrod—Tata McGraw Hill—2002.
2. *Principle of Genetics 7e* by Robert H. Tamarin, Tata McGraw Hill—2002.
3. A.J.F. Griffiths, J.H. Miller, D.T. Suzuki, R.C. Lewontin & W.M. Gelbart 2000. *An Introduction to genetic analysis,* 7th edition, Freeman, New York.
4. P.A. Hpffee, 1998, *Medical Molecular Genetics,* first edition, Fnce Creek Publishing, Madison.
5. *Basic Genetics, 2e* by Weaver, McGraw-Hill, 1995.
6. *Molecular Genetics* by S.R. Molay, J.E. Cronan, D. Friefelder, 1994, Jones and Bartlett Publishers.
7. *Molecular Genetics of Bacteria* by J.W. Datte, 1994, Wiley and Sons.
8. *Basic Genetics* by D.L.G. Hartl. 1991, Jones and Publishers.
9. *Principles of Genetics* by Gardner, Simmons and Snustad, 1991.
10. *Genetics* by Sarin—Tata McGraw-Hill, 1991.

PAPER 3
MOLECULAR CELL BIOLOGY

Unit-I

The dynamic cell—the molecules of life—the architecture of cells—the lifecycle of cells—cells into tissues—molecular cell biology. Protein structure and function—Hierarchical structure of proteins—folding modification and degradation of proteins—functional design of proteins—membrane proteins—purifying—detecting and characterizing proteins.

Unit-II

Nucleic acids, the genetic code, and the synthesis of macromolecules—structure of nucleic acids—synthesis of biopolymers—nucleic acid synthesis—the three roles of RNA in protein synthesis—stepwise formation of proteins on ribosome's. Biomembranes and the sub-cellular organisation of eukaryotic cells—microscopy and cell architecture—purification of cells and their parts—biomembranes—organelles of the eukaryotic cell.

Unit-III

Molecular structure of genes and chromosomes—molecular definition of a gene-chromosomal organisation of genes and noncoding DNA—mobile DNA functional rearrangements of chromosomal DNA organizing cellular DNA into chromosomes morphology and functional elements of eukaryotic chromosomes—organelle DNA's. Regulation of transcription initiation—bacterial gene control—bacterial transcription initiation—Eukaryotic gene control—regulatory sequence in eukaryotic protein-coding genes—eukaryotic transcription activators and repressors—RNA polymerase II transcription—Initiation complex-molecular mechanisms of eukaryotic transcriptional control.

Unit-IV

RNA processing—nuclear transport and post-transcriptional control—DNA replication—repair—recombination—regulation of eukaryotic cell—Gene control in development—transport across cell membranes—cellular energetics-glycolysis—aerobic oxidation—photosynthesis—protein sorting—organelle biogenesis—protein secretion—cell motility and shape I—microfilaments—cell motility and shape II—microtubules and intermediate filaments—cell to cell signalizing hormones and receptors—cell interaction in development.

Unit-V

Transcriptional and transnational controls; Regulation of gene expression in eukaryotic systems; Hormones and gene expression; Viruses and gene expression.

Growth factors; Mitogens and oncogenes; cellular regulation, development and differentiation, Genecontrol in development—myogenesis in mammals—neurognesis in Drosophila and Mice—Regional specification to the lifecycle and molecular biology of some important pathogen of AIDS, Malaria, Hepatitis, Tuberculosis, Filaria, Kalaazar.

REFERENCES

1. *Molecular Biology, 2e* by Weaver, McGraw Hill, 2002.
2. Lodish, H., Berk, A. Zipursky, S.L. Matsudaria, P. Baltimore, D. and Darnell, J. 2002, *Molecular Cell Biology,* Media Connected, W.H. Freeman and Company.
3. *Introduction to Molecular Biology,* Peter Paoleila—McGraw Hill, 1998.

PAPER 4
MICROBIOLOGY

Unit-I

History and Scope of Microbiology—Milestones in Microbiology—Recent developments and future trends. Basic Microbiology—Anatomy of Prokaryotes and Eukaryotes—Morphology—Ultra structure of Bacteria, Fungi, Algae, Protozoa and Viruses—structure and functions of the cellular components. Physiology—Growth and nutrition—nutritional requirements—kinetics of growth—media and culture.

Unit-II

Systematics and taxonomy—Classification of microbes—Phenotypic and taxonomic characters—Principles of classification—taxonomic structure—DNA analysis, Ribosomal RNA analysis—Numerical taxonomy—Molecular taxonomy—methods of microbial identification.

Unit-III

Applied Microbiology: Environment Microbiology—Microbial ecology—role of micro-organisms in the productivity of ecosystems—Interactions between micro-organisms and with plants and animals—microbes and biodeterioration—microbes in waste treatment. Food and Dairy Microbiology—Microbes in food—Role of Micro-organisms food production; dairy and non-dairy products fermented food and alcoholic beverages.

Unit-IV

Medical Microbiology—Pathogenic Microbes—Bacterial, Viral, Fungal and Protozoan diseases. Cure control and prevention, Industrial Microbiology—Industrial use of microbes—fermentation products—bioconversions—bioremediation, product of industrial microbiology, Penicillin, ethanol, vinegar, vitamin B12, citric acid and glutamic and protease etc.

Unit-V

Microbiology and Biotechnology—Biotechnological potentials of microbes—production of food (single cell protein), fuel (ethanol), pharmaceuticals (antibiotics, vaccines etc.), biofertilisers (BGA), biopesticides (Bacillus thuriensis), biopolymers, biosurfactants etc., biology of micro-organisms of importance and use in Biotechnology—Streptomyces, yeasts (Saccharomyces, Hansenula), Spirulina and Penicillium etc. Disposal of Microbes and Biosafety—(Environmental Microbiology Bioremediation).

REFERENCES

1. *Microbiology—Concepts and Applications,* Pelczar, M.J., Chan, E.C.S., King, N.R. McGraw-Hill, Inc. NY.
2. *Microbiology,* Prescott, L.M., Haley, J.P., Klecin, D.A., WCB Publishers, Sydney.
3. *Microbiology,* Davis, B.D., Dulbecco, R., Eisen, H.N., Gihsbercs, H.S., Harper and Row Publishers, Singapore.

4. L.A. Shimeld and A.T. Rodgers, *Essential of Diagnostic Microbiology*, Dilmer Publishers.
5. J.L. Ingraham and C.A. Ingraham, 2000. *Introduction to Microbiology*, 2nd edition, Brooks/Cole Thomson Learning, USA.
6. Kathleen Part Tolaro & A. Tolaro 1999, *Foundation of Micro Biology*, 3rd edition, McGraw-Hill
7. J.G. Cappuccino & N. Sharma, 1999, *Microbiology, A laboratory manual*, 4th edition, Wesley Longman Daniel Lim., 1998. *Microbiology*, 2nd edition McGraw-Hill.
8. *Principles of Microbiology*, 1997, RM Atlas, WCB Publishers.
9. A.M. Atlas and L.C. Parks, 1997, *Handbooks of Microbiology Media*, 2nd edition, CRC Press.

PAPER 5
PRACTICAL I
BIOCHEMISTRY AND BIOMOLECULES, MOLECULAR GENETICS, MOLECULAR CELL BIOLOGY

Biochemistry and Biomolecules

Calorimetry, Spectrophotometry and pH meters and buffers: Their theory and application Protein estimations Lowry and Brandford methods. Chromatography : A theoretical study of Gel filtration chromatography—Ion-exchange chromatography, Affinity chromatography, Thin layer chromatography (ILC), High performance liquid chromatography and Gas liquid chromatography and their demonstration, Production of extra cellular enzyme from the yeast and down stream processing—Ammonium Sulphate precipitation—ultrafilteration—Dialysis-ion-exchange, gel permeation etc.—Polyacrylamide gel electrophoresis, Radioactive labelling tracer techniques, measurement of radioactivity and autoradiography (Demonstration).

Molecular Genetics

Isolation of genomic DNA; Southern blotting; RFLP analysis; isolation of RNA; Isolation of poly A+ RNA; Northern blotting; Preparation of probes; *In vitro* transcription; Metabolic labelling of proteins and immunoprecipitation.

Molecular Cell Biology

Microscopy : Bright field, Phase contrast and Fluorescence microscopy, microtomy, Instrumental methods for cell biology; subcellular fraction and marker enzymes; Histochemical methods; mitosis and meiosis. Preparation of metaphae chromosomes from cultured cells; Isolation of DNA and demonstration of apoptosis of DNA laddering; MTT assay for cell viability and growth; cell fusion with PEG.

REFERENCES

1. *Molecular Biology, 2e* by Weaver, McGraw-Hill, 2002.
2. R. Rapley and J.M. Walker, 1998, *Molecular Biomethods Handbooks*, Humana Press.
3. *Microbial Genetics* by S.R. Maloy; J.E. Cronan, D. Friefelder (1994) Jone and Bartlett Publishers.

SEMESTER II

PAPER 6

BIOPHYSICS, BIOSTATISTICS AND COMPUTER APPLICATION

Unit-I

Introduction of digital computers; organisation; low-level and high-level languages; binary number systems; flow charts and programming techniques. Introduction to programming in Q Basic and C Introduction to data structures and database concepts, introduction to Internet and its applications.

Unit-II

Introduction to MS-Office software, covering Word Processing, Spreadsheets and presentation software—Introduction to Haward Graphics/Corel Draw—Computer oriented Statistical

Techniques—Frequency table of single discrete variable, bubble sort. Computation of mean, variance and standard deviation; t-test, correlation coefficient, bio-informatics and biotechnology.

Unit-III

Macromolecules and supra molecular assemblies—Type of macromolecules in biological systems, molecular assemblies like membranes, ribosome's, extra cellular matrix. Physical techniques in protein, nucleic acids and polysaccharide structural analysis (UV-IR, NMR-LASER, Raman, Spectroscopy MASS, Spectroscopy—Florescence Spectroscopy), Differential calorimetery—X-ray—Crystallography—Ultra-centrifugation—Electron Cryomicroscopy—Scanning Tunneling microscopy.

Unit-IV

Sequencing of proteins and nucleic acids—Protein—protein and protein-ligand interactions, physical and chemical methods for study. Conformational properties of polynuleotides and polysaccharides—secondary and tertiary structural features and their analysis—theoretical and experimental; protein folding—biophysical and cellular aspects. Protein and nucleic acid databases; structural comparison at secondary and tertiary levels.

Unit-V

Physical and chemical methods for immobilization of small and macromolecules. Glyco- and lipo-proteins—structure and function. Organisation of macromolecular complexes—chromatin and ribosome's protein denaturation—Nucleic acid hybridization—structural analysis and biological studies.

Unit-VI

Ribozymes and catalytic antibodies—functional proteins—structure and drug targets (enzymes and receptors)—Computer aided drug designing, computational techniques in structural analysis; nanoparticles.

REFERENCES

1. *Proteins—Structure and Moleular Properties,* TE, Creighton, WH. Freeman and Company.
2. *Introduction to Protein Structure,* C. Branden and J. Tooze, Garland Publishing, New York.
3. *Physical Chemistry of Macromolecules,* Tanford, C. John Wiley and Sons.
4. *Biophysical Chemistry,* Cantor, WH Freeman.

PAPER 7
MICROBIAL BIOPROCESS TECHNOLOGY

Unit-I

Enzyme and cell immobilization: methods of immobilization, electrostatic and external mass transfer effect on immobilisation, internal mass transfer effects on immobilisation.

Unit-II

Microbial growth kinetics: Monod growth kinetics, other forms of growth kinetics, unstructured and structured model of growth kinetics, product formation kinetics, cell destruction kinetics.

Unit-III

Bioreactor : batch reactors feed batch reactor, continuous stirred tank reactor with and without cell recycle, plug flow reactor, enzyme reactors, reactor dynamics and stability, non-ideal reactor and residence time distribution, mixing pattern.

Unit-IV

Sterilization and transport process: batch and continuous sterilization by filtration thermal death kinetics, gas liquid mass transfer in bioreactors, mass balance for two-phase bioreactor, mass transfer coefficient and is estimation, power requirement of bioreactors, scaling up, bubble column bioreactor, animal and plant cell bioreactors.

Unit-V

Production of some industrially important bioproducts; citric acid fermentation, penicillin production, production of anticancer agents, steroid fermentation brewing biotechnology, enzyme fermentation production of fermented dairy products, fermentation of biopolymers and amid acts, Downstream processing.

Mixed growth kinetics; neutralism, mutualism, communalism and amensalism, dynamics of two species growth, competition and selection, Lotka Volterra model and other prey and predator models, population dynamics.

REFERENCES

1. P.C. Trivedi, 2000, *Plant Biology : Recent Advancies,* PANIMa Publishing Corporation.
2. Sambrock *et al.,* 2000. *Molecular Cloning: a laboratory,* Manual, Cold SPRING Harbour Laboratory Press.
3. *Industrial Microbiology* by Casida (1997).
4. *Bio-reactor systems design* Ed. by J.A. Asenjo & J.C. Merchuk (1995).
5. *Plants, genes and agriculture* by M.J. Chrispeels and D.F. Sadava (1994), Jhones and Bartlett.
6. *Genetic Engineering of crop plants* by (Eds) G.W. Lycett and D. Grierson (1990).
7. *Plant Molecular Biology* by Grierson and S.N. Convey (1998), Blackie.
8. *Fundamentals of Biotechnology* by P. Prave, V. Faust W. Sitting and D.A. Sukatseh (Editors) (1987), WCH Weinhein.
9. *Comprehensive Biotechnology,* Volumes 2, 3 and 4 by M. Moo-young (Editior)(1985), Pergamon Press.
10. *Principles of Fermentation Technology* by P.F. Stanbury and A. Whitaker (1984), Pergamon Press.
11. *Chemical Engineering* by J.M. Coulson and J.F. Racjordson (1984), Pergamon Press.
12. *Papers* from Applied and Environmental Microbiology.
13. Papers from Biotechnology.

PAPER 8
ANIMAL CELL BIOLOGY

Unit-I

History of animal Biotechnology—Basic principles of biotechnology as applicable to animal Sciences Artificial Insemination, Pregnancy diagnosis, *In vitro* fertilization—Embryo Transfer Technology—Transgenic Animals.

Unit-II

Anima Health-Disease Diagnosis, Hybridoma Technique, Monoclonal antibodies, application of Probes for diagnosis of existing and emerging Animal diseases. Prophylaxis—Vaccines—Oral Vaccines—Modern Biotechnology Oriented Vaccines—DNA Vaccines in Animal disease. *In situ* PCR perside Digagnostic hits based on monoclonal antibodies. Oral vaccines—Enzymes in Animal Feed—Manipulation of rumen microbes.

Unit-III

Cell culture Technologies : Setting up of new cell culture laboratory—Adaptation of mammalian cell to growth in serum-free media—Viral evaluation of animal cell lines used Biotechnology—Molecular methods; Optimizing gene expression in mammalian cell—Cytogenetic characterization of Recombinant cells—Immortalization strategies for mammalian cells—Mouse monoclonal antibodies; immunization and production protocols—Cell Bank Preparation and characterization; DNA fingerprinting and characterization of animal cells—cell evaluation protocols: Cell counting and viability measurements—Monitoring animal cell growth and productivity—Measurement of cell death in culture—hollow film technology.

Unit-IV

Nuclear magnetic resonance methods of monitoring cell metabolism—Culturing animal cell in Fluidised bed reactors—GPI-Anchored fusion proteins—Harvesting GPI-Anchored Proteins from CHO cells—Hematopoietic cell for cellular and gene therapy.

Unit-V

Basic assay techniques—Expansion protocols—Cytotoxicity testing using cell lines—Product evaluation protocols. Measuring the folding dynamics of recombinant proteins secreted from mammalian cells—Control of proteolysis in cell culture : use of inhibitors and engineered cell lines—Monitoring recombinant Glyco-protein heterogeneity—Measurement of cell culture glycosidase activity.

REFERENCES

1. *Biotechnology* by Trevan—Tata McGraw- Hill, 2001.
2. *Biology and Biotechnology Science, Applications, and Issues,* H. Kreuzer & A. Massey, American Society for Microbiology (2005).
3. J.M. Walker and E.B. Gingold, 1999, *Molecular Biology and Biotechnology,* 3rd edition, Panima Publishing Corp.
4. Nigel Jenkins (Ed), 1990, *Animal Cell Biotechnology : Methods and Protocols,* Human Press, New Jersey, pp. 1-302.
5. *Basic Biotechnology* by Ignacimuthu, Tata McGraw-Hill, 1996.
6. J.D. Watson, M. Gillman, J. Witknowski and M. Zoller (1992), *Recombinant DNA* (2nd Ed), Scientific American Books, NY.
7. *Genetic Engineering of Animals* (Ed.) A. Puhler (1993), VCH Publishers, Weinheim, FRG, Human Press.
8. *Gene Transfer and Expression Protocols—Methods in Molecular Biology* Vol. 7 by ET. Murray (1991), Humana Press.
9. *Molecular Biology of Gene* by J.D. Watson, N.H. Hopkins, J.M. Roberts, J.A. Steitz and A.M. Weiner (1987), Benjamin/Cummings 4th Ed. Vol. 1&2.

PAPER 9
PLANT BIOTECHNOLOGY

Unit-I

Plant genome organisation, structure of representative plant genes and gene families in plants organisation of chloroplast genome, nuclear encoded and chloroplast encoded genes for chloroplast proteins, targeting of proteins to chloroplast.

Unit-II

Organisation of mitochondrial genome—encoded genes for mitochondrial proteins—RNA edition for plant mitochondria—cytoplasmic male sterility—Seed storage proteins—maize transposable elements—their organisation and function, transposable elements in transgenic plants—Regulation of gene expression in plant development—Plant hormones and phytochrome.

Unit-III

Transgenic plants and applications—vaccine (Plantbodies) and other biological development: Inducible control of gene expression: an overview—Use of the TN10-encoded tetracycline repression to control gene expression—Ecdysteroid against—inducible control of gene expression in plants.

Unit-IV

Glusocorticoid—inducible gene expression in plants—Tissue—specific, copper—controllable gene expression in plants—Nitrate inducibility of gene expression using the nitrite reductase gene promoter—use of heat shock promoters to control gene expression in Plants-wound—inducible genes in plants.

Unit-V

Development of targets of gene expression by the use of Senescence—specific promoter—Abseisic of acid—and stress—induced promoter switches in the control of gene expression—Potential use of hormone responsive elements to control gene expression in plants.

REFERENCES

1. Kojima, Hiroyuki Lee, Y. Kun, 2001, *Photosynthesis Microorganisms in Environmental Biotechnology*, Springer, Verlag.
2. M. Sudhir, 2000, *Applied Biotechnology & Plant Genetics*, Dominant Publisher and Distributors.
3. P.C. Trivedi, 2000, *Plant Biotechnology : Recent Advances*, PANIMa Publishing Corporation.
4. Reynolds, P.H.S. (Ed), 1999 *Inducible Gene Expression in Plants*, CABI Publishing, U.K.
5. *Applied : Plant Biotechnology by Ignacimuthu*, Tata McGraw-Hill, 1996.
6. *Plants, Genes and Agriculture* by M.J. Chrispeels and D.F. Sadava (1994), Jhones and Bartlett.
7. *Genetic Engineering of Crop Plats* by (Eds) G.W. Lycett and D. Grierson (1990).
8. *Plant Molecular Biology* by Grierson and S.N. Convey (1986) Blackie.

PAPER 10
PRACTICAL II
ANIMAL CELL BIOTECHNOLOGY, MICROBIAL BIO PROCESS TECHNOLOGY, PLANT BIOTECHNOLOGY

Animal Cell Biotechnology

Preparation of tissue culture medium and membrane filtration; preparation of single cell suspension from spleen and thymus; cell counting and cell viability; Macrophage monolayer form PEC and measurement of phagocytic activity; Trypsinization of monolayer and subculturing; Cryopreservation and thawing measurement of doubling time; Role of serum in cell culture.

Micro Bio-Process Technology

Bio-processing in the lab using bioreactors (batch and continuous bio-processing)—Lab fermentation of antibiotics—Efficient recovery of the products—Gene manipulation to produce microbes for the production of antobiotics in the laboratory experimental bioreactors—use of plasmids, phages, restriction enzymes, gene mapping and use of pulse field electrophoresis in gene mapping.

Isolation of industrially important micro-organisms for microbial processes; Determination of thermal death point (TDP) and thermal death time (TDT) of micro organisms for design of a sterilizer; Determination of growth curve of a supplied microorganism and also determine substrate degradation profile; compute specific growth rate (m), growth yield ($Y_{x/s}$) from the above; Experiment; Comparative studies of Ethanel production using different substrates; Microbial production of Citric acid using Aspergillus niger; Microbial production of antibiotics (Penicillin); Production and estimation of Alkaline protease; Sauer Krant fermentation; Use of alginate for cell immobilisation.

Plant Biotechnology

On hand training in cell and tissue culture and maintenance of culture lines—Callus propagation of plants—Electroporation—Biolistic transformation (Demonstration)—Southern and Northern hybridization.

Preparation of media; Surface sterilization; organogenesis, transfer of plants to soil; Protoplast isolation and culture; Anther culture, production of Haploids; Cytological examination of regenerated plants; Agrobacterium culture, selection of transformants, reporter gene (GUS) assays; Developing RFLP and RAPD maps.

REFERENCES

1. M. Sudhir, 2000, *Applied Biotechnology & Plant Genetics,* Dominant Publishers and Distributions.

2. Reynolds P.H.S (Ed) 1999. *Inducible gene expression in plants.* CABI Publishing, U.K. pp. 1-247.
3. *Gene transfer and expression protocols—Methods in Molecular biology* Vol.7 by ET Murrary (1991) Human Press.

SEMESTER III
PAPER 11
CLONING VECTORS

Unit-I

Genome—Replication—Transcription—Translation in Prokaryotes and Eukaryotes—Recombination and Repair—Restricution Endonucleases—properties—functions—ligation of DNA fragments—E.Coli vectors.

Unit-II

Plasmid biology—pBR 322 and its derivatives—gene markers—Cloning vectors for gram—negative bacteria and phage—filamentous phages—Cosmid—Phasmid Cloning in Gram—Positive Bacteria Bacillus subtillis—transformation techniques—Gene expression in eukaryotes.

Unit-III

Cloning in Yeast—Saccharomyces cerevisiae genetics—lifecycle types of vectors—gene expression sustem—Eukaryotic Vectors—SV40—molecular gentics—markers—expression systems—Clonin and gene expression in Streptomyces.

Unit-IV

Specialised cloning vectors for cDNA—synthesis of specific RNA *in vitro*—selection of vectors for copy number—cloning promoters and Terminator—Plant cloning vectors—Agrobacterium tumefaciens—plasmics—molecular genetics and gene expression.

Unit-V

Animal cell cloning vectors—Baculoviruses—mammalian expression vectors—retroviral vectors—Expression vectors for fusion proteins—promoters—translation—protease—gene fusion—secretion—modification and protein refolding—inducible/constitutive expression cassettes—Sub-cloning of genes—vectors for sub-cloning—Identification of rDNA—Impact of gene cloning and Bioethics.

REFERENCES

1. *Vectors—A survey of Molecular cloning vectors and their uses*—Raymond L. Rodriguez, David T. Denhart.
2. *From Genes to clones—Introduction to Gene Technology,* Errst-L. Winnacker.
3. *Gene expression technology Methods in enzymology* (vol. 185)—ed. David V. Goeddel.
4. *Priciples of Gene Manupulation: An Introduction to Genetic Engineering,* R.W. Old & S.B. Primrose.
5. *Methods in Gene Biotechnology,* William Wu, Michal J. Welsh, Peter B. Kaufrmar, Helen H. Zhang.
6. *Maximizing Gene Expression*, by William Rezmikff, Lamy Gold.
7. C.J.A. Ring & E.D. Blair, 2001, *Genetically Engineered Viruses: Development and Application.*

PAPER 12
GENETIC ENGINEERING

Unit-I

The concept of genes—molecular anatomy of eukaryotic genes-control of gene expression—recombinant DNA technology—fundamental principles of cloning—vectors for use in plant and animal cells.

Unit-II

Principal genomic and cDNA cloning strategies—genetically

modified micro-organisms—plant, animals molecular techniques in prenatal diagnosis—systic fibrosis, muscular dystrophies, Huntington's disease coronary heart disease, microbial infections—Recombinant DNA methods in vaccine development—molecular diagnosis of cancer—gene therapy—protein engineering.

Unit-III

Genetic engineering and rDNA technology—genetic complexity—enzymes used in gene manipulation of DNA, RNA—restriction endonucleases—molecular scalpels—isolation and purification of plasmid DNA—isolation of mRNA from mammalian cells.

Unit-IV

Autoradiography—electrophoresis of DNA—plused field gel electrophoresis (PFGE)—Nucleic Acid staining—Nucleic Acid labelling—molecular probes—hydridization techniques—DNA finger printing—(DNA profiling)—Restriction fragment length polymorphism (RFLP)—Blotting Techniques—vectors-Gene cloning—Screening and analysis of Recombinants—protoplast Technology—fusion techniques—DNA-protein interactions—DNA libraries—Chromosome walking and chromosome walking and jumping-site diected mutagenesis—DNA synthesis—techniques of gene mapping ribozyme.

Unit-V

Polymerase chain reaction (PCR)—Random amplification of polymorphic DNA (RAPD)—substraction hybridization—ribotyping—protein engineering-strain improvement—gene transfer technologies (DNA transfer methods)—transgenesis—Gene targeting—Antisense therapy—flow cytogenetics—genome projects—ethical, legal social, environmental and health issues related to gene biotechnology.

REFERENCES

1. *Gene cloning*—T.A. Brown.
2. *Principles of Gene Manipulation*—Old & Primrose.
3. *Biotechnology DNA to Protein: A Laboratory Project* by Thiel—Tata McGraw-Hill, 2002.
4. C.J.A. Ring and E.D. Blair, 2001, *Genetically Engineered viruses. Development and application.* Bios Scientific Publishers.
5. M.Walker & E.B.Ginglod,1999, *Molecular Biology and Biotechnology,* 3rd Panama Publishing Corp.

PAPER 13
IMMUNOTECHNOLOGY

Unit-I

Basic concepts in immunology : Antigen—Isolation, purification and characterization of various antigens and haptens from pathogens and other biological molecules by biophysical and chemical affinity separation methods.

Unit-II

Production of antibodies, purification of antibodies, Quantation of immunoglobulin by RID, EID and nephlometry.

Unit-III

Hybridoma and monoclonal antibody production, Immunodiagnosis and Application of monoclonal antibodies in biomedical research; human monoclonal antibodies; catalytic antibodies; complement fixation test; assessment of immue complexes in tissues.

Unit-IV

Purification of mononuclear cells from peripheral blood; isolation and characterization of T cell subsets; B cells and macrophages;

Fluroescent Activated Cell Sorter (FACS); Mitogen and Antigen induced Lympho—proliferation assay; cell mediated Lympholysis; Mixed Lymphocyte reaction; Assessment of delayed hypersensitivity reactions; Macrophage cultures; Assay for macrophage activation; Isolation of dendritic cells; *In vivo* characterization of cells from tissues; Generation of T cell clones; HLA typing.

Unit-V

Biology & assay of cytokines; Vaccine technology including DNA vaccines; Identification of T&B epitopes for vaccine development; immunotechnology and infectious diseases. Immunoscreening of recombinant library.

REFERENCES

1. Immunity and Inflammation by Ramasamy, P. & R.E.B. Hanna, 2002, University of Madras Publication, Pearl Press Ltd.
2. T.G. Parslow, D.P., Sities, A.L.Terr 2001, *Medical Immunology,* 10th edition McGraw-Hill.
3. H. Zola 2000, *Monoclonal antibodies,* Bios Scientific Publishers Ltd.
4. *Kuby Immunology* by R.A. Gold.
5. *Immunology* by I. Roitt (1996) Blackwell Scientific Publications.
6. *Current Protocols in Immunology,* 3 volumes, Wiley Publications, 1994.
7. *Immunological Techniques* by D.M. Weir (1992) 3 volumes. Blackwell Scientific Publication.

PAPER 14
ENZYME TECHNOLOGY

Unit-I

Enzyme nomenclature and classification; General proposals of enzymes and the factors that affect their activity and the associated changes; Extraction assay and purification of enzymes.

Unit-II

Enzyme kinetics (steady state), determination of Km value and studying kinetics using Lineweaver Burke plot, Eadie-Hofstee plot and Hans—Woolf equations—Enzymes inhibitors—Presteady state kinetics—fast kinetics to elucidate the intermediate and rate limiting steps (flow and relaxation techniques); complex kinetics and analysis; enzymes inhibitors.

Unit-III

Enzyme specificity—Evidences for enzyme substrate complex—Nucleophic and Electrophilic attack—Role of mental ions in enzyme catalysis; Mechanism of enzyme action (lyzozyme, chymotrypsin).

Unit-IV

DNA polymerase, RNase etc., zymogens and enzymes and enzyme activators, active site dtermination, Regulation of enzymes—allosteric interactions and product inhibition; Coenzymes, Isoenzymes and metalloenzymes.

Unit-V

Membrane bound enzymes—their extraction assay, lipid-protein interaction and the effect of fluidity on enzyme activity. Clinical and Industrial Applications of Enzymes—Immobilisation of enzymes—Enzyme engineering.

REFERENCES

1. *Biochemistry* by Voet & Voet.
2. *Enzymes* by Dixon & Webb.
3. *Immobilised Enzyme* by Messing.

PAPER 15
PRACTICAL-III
GENETIC ENGINEERING IMMUNOTECHNOLOGY, ENZYME TECHNOLOGY

Genetic Engineering

Cloning of DNA into expression vectors—transformation of microbes—Southern hybridization—Use of radioactive (Demonstration) and non-radioactive probes—S1 mapping—DNA sequencing—genomic DNA isolation from microbes/animals/plants—Site directed mutagenesis and PCR; Electrophoresis of DNA—linear, circular and super coiled; protein—DNA interactions Nucleic acid hybridization; Determination of TM of nucleic acid.

Bacterial culture and antibiotic selection media. Preparation of competent cells; isolation of plasmid DNA; Isolation of lambda phage DNA; Quantitiation of nucleic acids; Agarose gel electrophoresis and restriction mapping of DNA; construction of restriction map of plasmid DNA; cloning in plasmid/phagemid vectors; Preparation of helper phage and its titration; preparation of single stranded DNA template; DNA sequencing; Gene expression in E. Coli and analysis of gene product; PCR; Reporter Gene assay (Gus CAT /b-GAL).

Immunotechnology

Separation of lymphocytes (lymphoprep /Ficol hypoprep)—T&B lymphocytes differentiation—immunoglobulin preparation use of sephadex colours for deportation of immunoglobulins–n development-conjugates—lymphoid organs and their microscopic organization; immunization; collection of Serun; Double diffusion.

Enzyme Technology

Electrophoresis of proteins—native and under denaturing conditions; N and C terminal analysis of proteins; Peptide mapping

Separation technologies (HPLC, GPC, FPLC); Chemical modification of proteins; Enzyme; purification and kinetic analysis; Hydro-dynamic properties—measurement and application; Methods for immobilisation of enzymes; Techniques for analysis of secondary, tertiary and quaternary structures of proteins.

REFERENCES

1. *Gene cloning*—T.A. Brown.
2. *Principles of Gene Manipulation*—Old & Primrose.
3. *Current protocols in Immunology,* 3 Volumes, Wiley Publication, 1994.
4. *Immunological techniques* by D.M. Weir (1992), 3 Volumes, Blackwell Scientific Publication.
5. *Immobilised Enzymes* by Messing.

SEMESTER—IV
PAPER 16
TISSUE ENGINEERING

Unit-I

Tissue engineering in perspective : thc basis of growth and differentiation—morphogenesis and tissue engineering.

Unit-II

In vitro control of tissue development—Growth factors—Tissue engineering bioreactors—Tissue assembly in microgravity—*In vitro* synthesis of Tissue and Organs—Organotypic and histotypic models of engineered tissues.

Unti-III

Biomaterials in tissue engineering—Approaches to transplanting engineered cells and tissues—Engineering challenges in immunosisation device development—Fetal tissue engineering—Breast reconstruction—Small diameter vascular grafts—Cardic prostheses.

Unit-IV

Bioartificial pancreas—Hepatassist liver support systems—Heamatopoietic systems: Red Blood Cell substitutes—Rental replacement devices—Musculoskeletal system : Structural tissue engineering.

Unit-V

Bone regeneration through cellular engineering—Brain implants—Neural stem cell—Periodontal application—Regeneration of Dentin skin—Wound repair : Basic biology to tissue engineering—Artificial Womb.

REFERENCE

Robert P. Lanaza, Robert Langer and Joseph Vacanti (Eds.) (2000), *Principles of Tissue Engineering,* Second edition, Academic Press, pp. 1-999.

PAPER 17
GENOICS AND PROTEOMICS

Unit-I

Genomic and cDNA sequences and output management from different biological output sources gene prediction rules and software.

Unit-II

Human Genome Project—Mutations, Population Studies—Gene therapy, Analysis of genomic and proteomic information with respect to biological systems—Genome Applications—Transgenic animals and plants—Pathway regulatory networks. Drug designing/ discovery and identification, synthesis of new drugs—Management of diverse chemicals libraries.

Unit-III

Gene expression : Microarrays and recent developments in expression analysis : Genes; Oncogenes—Proto Oncogenes—Classification of Cancer Types : Applications of Microarrays in Drug Toxicity Testing, Metabolic Pathways.

Unit-IV

Sequence analysis (Proteins and Nucleic Acids) Sequence Alignment methods—Proteomics : Proteins Analysis—Structural Comparisons—2 D gel, Mass Spec, Proteins and Antibody arrays Proteins Databases Comparison of Protein sequences and Database searching.

Unit-V

Methods for Protein Structure Prediction—conserved Patterns in Protein sequences and structures comparison of Protein 3D structures—Predicting Functions based DNA and Protein sequences.

REFERENCES

1. Malcolm & J. Goodship, 2001, *Genotype to phenotype,* 2nd edition, Bio Scientific Publishers Ltd.
2. S.B. Primrose, 1998, *Principle of genome analysis,* 2nd edition, Blackwell Science.

PAPER 18
ENVIRONMENTAL BIOTECHNOLOGY

Unit-I

Biofilm kinetics, Completely mixed biofilm reactor—Soluble microbial products and inert biomass—special case biofilm solutions.

Unit-II

Reactors : Reactor types—A batch reactor—A continuous flow stirred—tank reactor with effluent recycle—A Plug—flow reactor—A plug flow reactor with effluent recycles—Reactors with recycle of settled cells using alternate rate models—Linking stoichio-metric equations to mass balance equations—Engineering design of reactors—Reactors in series.

Unit-III

Denitrification : Physiology of denitrifying bacteria—Tertiary denitrification—one—sludge denitrification—Drinking water treatment : Anaerobic treatment by methanogenesis uses for methanogenic treatment—Reactor configurations—Special factors for the design of anaerobic sludge digesters.

Unit-IV

Dettoxification of Hazardous chemicals : Factors causing molecular recalcitrance—Synthetic organic chemical classes—Energy metabolism versus co-metabolism—electron donor versus electron acceptor—Minimum substrate concentration (Sm/n) Biodegradation of problem environmental contaminants.

Unit-V

Bioremediation : Engineering strategies for bioremediation—Evaluating bioremediaton—Sewage and waste treatment—Pollution monitoring, control and remediation (petroleum industry, paper industry, chemical industry etc.) Biogas—Biomass from the wastes.

REFERENCES

1. Bruce E. Rittmann and Perry L. McCarty 2001, *Environmental Biotechnology: Principles and Application,* McGraw-Hill, New York, pp. 1-754.
2. A. Ahmed, F.M. Qureshi and O.Y. Khan 2001, *Industrial Environmental Biotechnology,* Horizon Press.

PAPER 19
BIOETHICS, BIOSAFETY, IPR, HUMAN RIGHTS AND SOCIAL ISSUES

Unit-I

Introduction : Historical Development of Human Rights and Relations—International and National.

Unit-II

International Instruments : United Commission for Human Rights, European Convention for Human Rights, UDHR, Civil and Political Rights, National Instruments : National and State Instrument Development of Human Rights—Article 21 of Constitution of India.

Unit-III

Human Relations : Political relations, ethnic and communal relations, socio-cultural relations organisation relation etc. and related Human Rights—Economics of Human Rights and Relations.

Unit-IV

Adam Smiths thoughts on moral sentiments—Economic Philosophy of Thiruvallur.

Students Activity : Assignment/Case study/Term Paper etc.

Unit-V

Impact on gene cloning and Bioethics, Intellectual Property Rights (IPR) and patents, biosafety containment facilities for Genetic Engineering experiments, Regulations on field experiments and release of GMO's (Genetically Modified Organisms), labelling of GM (Genetically Modified) foods.

REFERENCES

1. Vadakar Praveen, *Concepts, Theories and Practices of Human Rights,* Rajat Publication, 2000.
2. Mishra, Pramod, *Human Rights Global Issues,* Kalpaz Publications—2000.
3. Paul, R.C. *Situations of Human Rights in India,* Efficient Offset Printers, 2000.
4. Marc Galanter, *Social Inequality.*
5. Adam Smith, *Theory of Moral Sentiments.*
6. Thiruvanuvar, *Thirukural : Arathuppal and Porutpal.*
7. Kretch & Crutchfield, *Social Psychology.*

PAPER 20
PRACTICAL—IV
ENVIRONMENTAL BIOTECHNOLOGY

Detection of coli forms for determination of purity of water, Detemination of total dissolved solids of water; Determination of dissolved oxygen concentration of water sample; determination of biological oxygen demand (BOD) of a sewage sample; Determination of chemical oxygen demand (COD) of sewage sample; Determine the efficiency of removal of air pollutant using fibrous air filter; isolation of xenobiont degrading bacterial by selective enrichment technique; Test for the degradation of a aromatic hydrocarbons by bacteria; Survey of degradative plasmids growing in polluted environment; Effect of sulphur dioxide on crop plants; Estimation of heavy metals in water/soil by atomic absorption spectrophotometer; estimation of nitrate in drinking water; study on biogenic methane production in different habitats.

REFERENCES

1. Moo-Young (Ed-in-Chief) *Comprehensive Biotechnology,* Vol. 4, Pergamon Press, Oxford.
2. De, A.K., *Environmental Chemistry,* Willey Eastern Ltd., New Delhi.
3. Metcalf Eddy, *Wastewater Engineering—Treatment, Disposal and Reuse.* Tata McGraw-Hill, New Delhi.

INDEX